"Great book, it will change your game forever! I recommend this book to every type of golfer. I went through the class with Scott, who opened my eyes to a lot about the game and made me realize I had been looking at it and thinking about it the wrong way. My handicap improved from +1 to +3.2 in 4 weeks!"

—Brent Boyles, Course Participant

The Champions Playbook

Scott Hassee, PGA

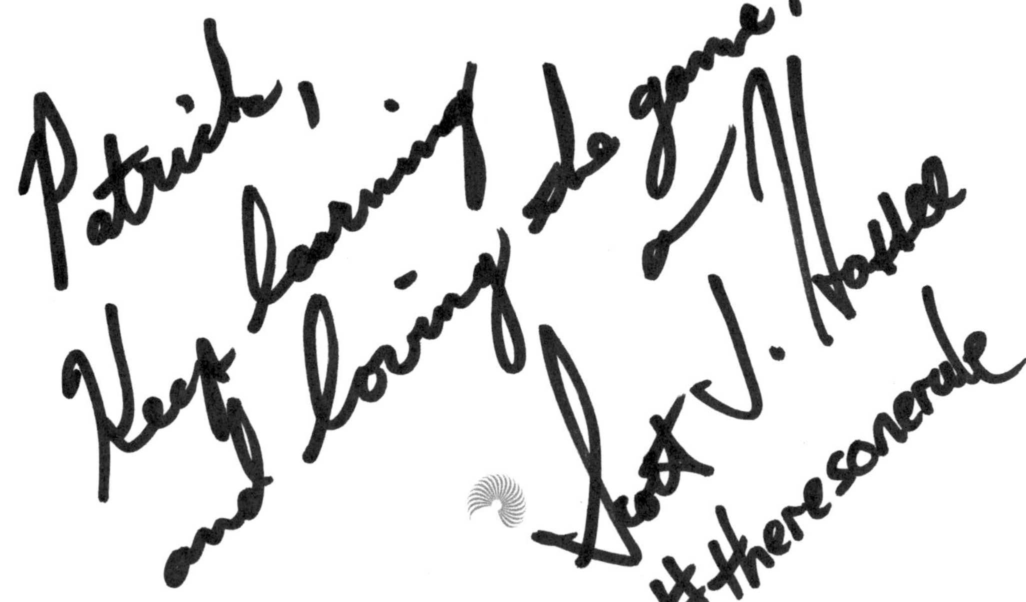

Cover and text design by Beth Farrell
Cover and text layout by Ann Forsyth

Sea Script Company
Seattle, Washington
www.seascriptcompany.com
206.390.6628
info@seascriptcompany.com

ISBN: 978-1-7335583-2-7
Library of Congress Control Number: 2019910577

First Printing September 2019

Printed in the United States

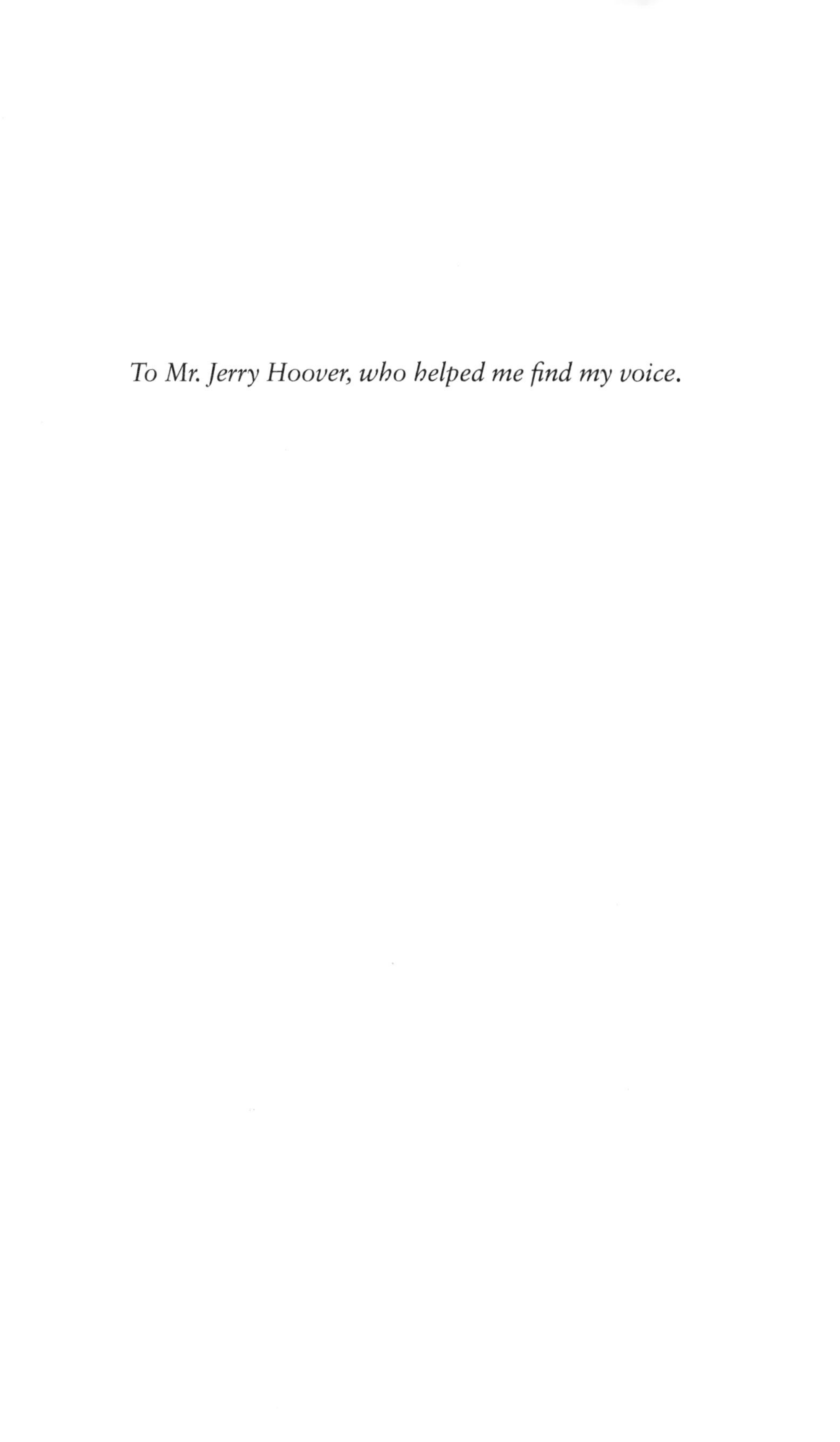

To Mr. Jerry Hoover, who helped me find my voice.

For more information about
Scott Hassee and
The Champions Playbook visit:
www.tcplaybook.com
Instagram: @tcplaybook
205.200.4686

To visit Scott's podcast:

https://www.podbean.com/ei/pb-r9t9u-b7d2b1

TABLE OF CONTENTS

Foreword: Hank Johnson

Introduction: Scott Hassee

Course One: What Do You Believe? 1

Course Two: Understanding the Architect 19

Course Three: Have a Plan 35

Course Four: Revising Your Plan 53

Course Five: Game Time Decision Making 67

Course Six: Developing Your Instincts 91

Course Seven: Mind Control 107

Final Exam: Go and Do It 119

Products 122

Acknowledgements 123

About the Author 125

Bibliography 127

FOREWORD

Golf is really a pretty simple game. How you do can be summed up in the answer to one basic question: What did you shoot?

If your primary objective is to shoot the lowest possible score each time you go out, then this book will be a significant and positive influence on your future success with your golf game. You will learn how to accurately assess your "Golf Tool Box"—the clubs and shots you are capable of playing successfully a reasonable percentage of the time. You will also learn how to accurately recognize and evaluate *the opportunities for scoring* that the golf course presents to you, as well as a process through which you can most accurately match your current scoring skills against *the defense* the golf course presents to you.

Most other sports are played on uniform playing fields that add a sameness to the game. Golf courses are anything but uniform. Because of this, in each round of golf the player is likely to encounter shots that are just a little different from others they had in the past. This requires the player to 1. create on-the-spot shots that are appropriate for the exact circumstances and challenges of each course played and 2. be capable of evaluating their own skills in that moment to fit the situation presented to them.

When asked how he prepared for a tournament, an old English professional named James Braid said four things:

1. Know the course.
2. Know the rules.
3. Know yourself.
4. Get on with it!

The Champions Playbook will help you do these things and more.

—Hank Johnson, PGA
2004 PGA National Teacher of the Year

INTRODUCTION

Golf is deceptively simple and endlessly complicated; it satisfies the soul and frustrates the intellect. It is at the same time rewarding and maddening—and it is without a doubt the greatest game mankind has ever invented.

—Arnold Palmer

This is one of the most famous quotes in golf by one of the greatest golfers of all time. The reason we recognize it is that it resonates with us. We have experienced the highs and lows of the game, the glories and defeats and, somehow, even in the depths of despair, we come crawling back to this rollercoaster of a game. I do believe, however, that I can turn your moments of despair into triumphs, and turn your triumphs into even more satisfying victories by changing how you see the game. For far too long, we have given ourselves over to our own devices and the clichés that are so pervasive in the golfing culture. It's time you learn to see the game as it truly is and develop the necessary skills to play your best golf in your own unique way!

I began writing this book a few years ago after watching, not only our students, but hundreds of golfers around my state continue to underperform with their skill set. This led them to feelings of frustration, disappointment, even anger and despair. It led to disillusionment about their own abilities, while further ingraining the behaviors that put them there in the first place!

There are exceptions, some golfers develop the necessary techniques on their own or they're "naturals" at strategy, yet they too are missing some key pieces of information. My passion for helping others led to writing this book and developing the exercises within to guide my students through these concepts. You will read stories of successes from players young and old who have shown great improvement just by applying these principles. I firmly believe that everyone who reads this book can play better golf and enjoy the game at a much deeper level than they ever have.

So what makes this book different than other course management books or programs out there? I teach the *principles* that underlie the game of golf, and then I teach you *how to think*, which allows you to solve any problem you encounter *while developing* your own unique instincts. Teaching course management in this way will change what you fundamentally *believe* about the game which, in turn, will affect the *behaviors* you exhibit on the course. Most books tell people *what to do* or they provide an extensive list of things to remember and leave you confused about where to start. Others ignore the "human factors" of personality, experience, feelings, and creativity thus downplaying the power of the human mind and instincts. In addition, course management has been historically taught by my fellow PGA golf professionals by playing nine or eighteen holes with a player (I was once one of them) and telling them what to do differently in specific circumstances.

I have a bachelor's degree in economics with a minor in mathematics. I've been teaching golf since 2010, learning from one of the finest golf instructors in the world, Hank Johnson. One thing you begin to understand in upper level mathematics is that you can't memorize all the answers in a textbook. It's essential that you seek to deeply understand the principles of the particular subject you study.

I remember early on Hank told me I wouldn't be able to memorize all the answers to fixing a golf swing. What I needed to do was watch, listen, imitate, and *develop my own instincts* as a teacher. I learned *how to think* through the errors of the student I was trying to help given the slew of factors involved.

We often sat at lunch discussing the morning lessons and, while we could understand why a certain thing worked for a player, Hank could not tell us *why* he chose to fix that thing a particular way other than, "It felt like the right thing to do." His mind works by understanding the principles that affect ball flight, motor learning, student motivation, and physical abilities in a way that only experience can teach you. There are too many answers to memorize, too many possibilities to face, so better to learn the *principles* of a thing in order to enjoy it, learn it, and improve.

After showing Hank notes I had written of my ideas a few years ago, he came back to me and said, "This is incredible, I've never seen anything like it in all my years of teaching." I subsequently put together a class at which I could teach a small group of students and test the validity of the concepts. The class provided me with both the evidence that it works and allowed me to make modifications to bring it to others. It was an immediate success, and in a fireside chat with members and students of our instruction program, Hank told the group,

"Scott doesn't know it yet, but he's going to turn this into a book one day." So here we are!

I have run this course several times and taught the principles in various individual contexts. To date, nearly every student, young and old, produced at least one personal best; a few won at least one tournament; and the average stroke improvement was more than three strokes in just a few short weeks from the start of the class. I'll share some of these stories as you read along.

A word about the structure of *The Champions Playbook*: It's a book about *doing something different,* as though you were actually attending one of my classes. Simply knowing more about golf won't affect the change in you that you desire. Some of my favorite course management books give you so much information that you're left knowing a lot more, forgetting more than you remember, and leave you wondering how to apply the information if you can at all! In the following pages, there are exercises in each chapter that are specifically designed to maximize your learning and are *essential* to playing your best golf. In order to receive the full benefit and impact of this book, it's best to complete the book.

I have included a section in each chapter for the "Advanced Player." This section is an effort to extend the same principles specifically to those who are high level amateur players or touring professionals. If you are able to consistently break 80 and have at least had some rounds at or below par, then this section is for you. Keep in mind that experience is a great teacher—the exercises, concepts, and methods presented serve to accelerate your application of these principles, improve the *quality* of your experience, and allow you to *develop your own instincts* as you continue to play for years to come.

For those who complete the reading and the exercises, I invite you to join me for a week-long course management class. If you are a high school coach, college coach, or a golf course or academy, I would love nothing more than to have the opportunity to provide tremendous value to your program, staff, or membership in a one- or two-day setting. I will extend these concepts, answer your questions, and guide you with individualized attention in a small class setting to help you lose those extra strokes. Open your mind, turn the page, and get ready to step up your game!

—Scott Hassee

www.tcplaybook.com

The Champions Playbook

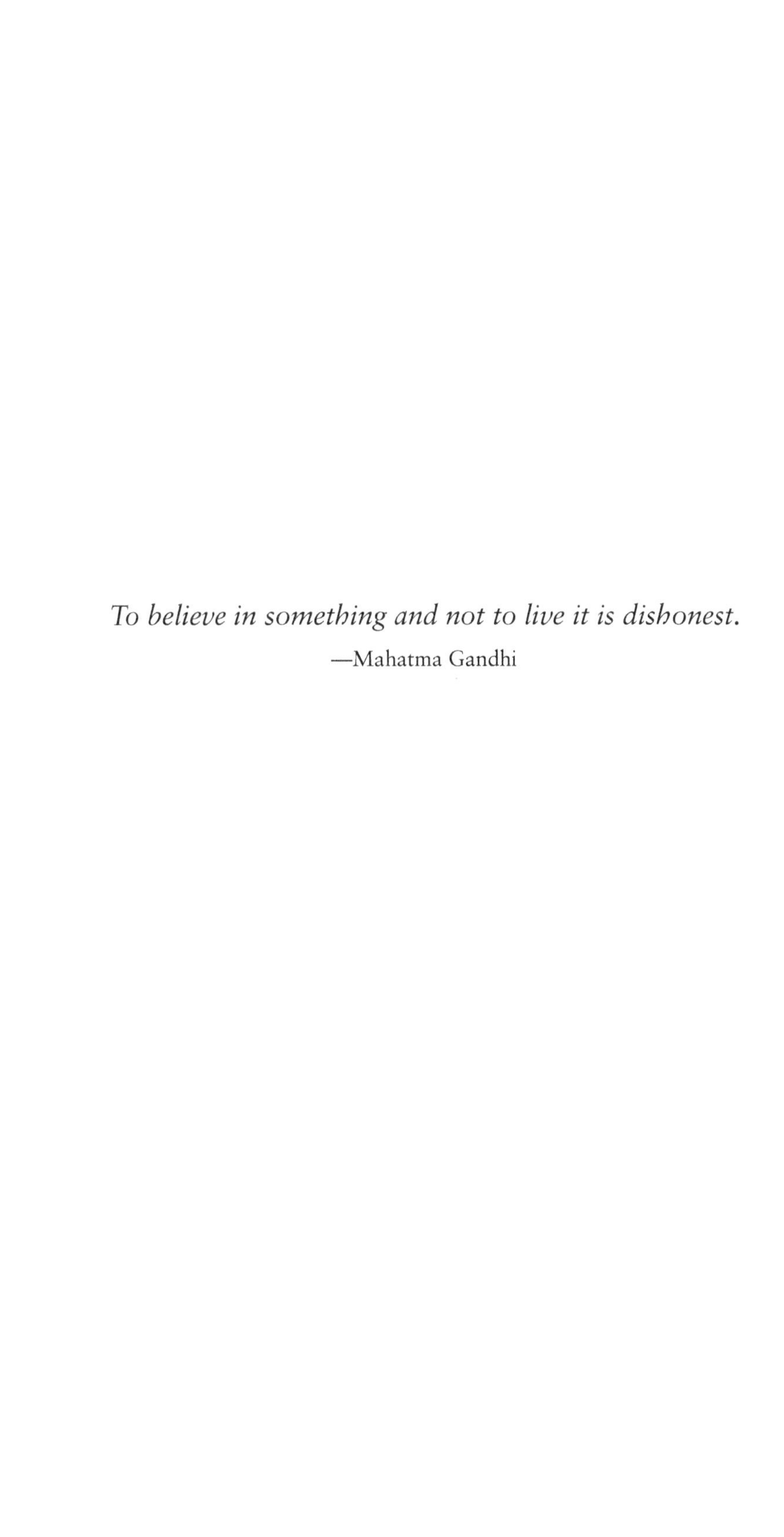

To believe in something and not to live it is dishonest.

—Mahatma Gandhi

COURSE ONE: WHAT DO YOU BELIEVE?

GOLF CAN BE SUMMARIZED IN ONE QUESTION: What did you shoot? After all, the object of the game is to shoot the lowest possible score. This may seem obvious, but it *must* govern every decision you make. Sadly, golfers tend to play with some other objective or obsessive impulse that is nothing more than a distraction. In this first course, I'll show you more specifically what I mean and how we got here. Let's get started!

What you *believe* affects how you *behave*. Let's first take a look at the behaviors that reveal our basic set of beliefs about the game.

Common phrases:

- "My coach, parents, caddy say I should. . ."
- "I just didn't hit it good."
- "I couldn't putt."
- "I can't hit it anywhere."
- "Nothing feels solid."
- "I hate playing this course, playing with so and so, etc."
- Other: ________________________

Common actions:

- o Trying to outdrive your buddies—or just hit it farther
- o Negative body language after bad shots
- o Punch it through a small opening
- o Playing the hole the same way as your competitors do
- o Firing at the flag
- o Shoot the distance, grab the club, swing with very little or no thought process
- o Other: ____________________________

There are certainly a number of thoughts, phrases, or actions that are not listed above that reflect a belief system not in line with the universal principle of shooting the lowest score. Take a few minutes to highlight the ones above that you fall prey to or list others that don't seem to align with this objective.

I have had many discussions with people who say that these words or actions had a positive effect on the score. While that may be true at times, getting the ball in the hole in the fewest strokes may have absolutely nothing to do with the items above. When people talk in generalities like this, they most often are looking at it from a heavily subjective, biased, and emotional viewpoint. For instance, I had several of my junior golfers walk in one day in 2016 and say, "Did you see Dustin Johnson hit that 420-yard drive yesterday?" to which I replied, "Yes, what did he make on the hole?" He made a par on a par 4 that left him less than 100 yards into the green. The point was this: Hitting it farther does not *guarantee* you shoot a lower score. In fact, a close female friend of mine was a good ball striker that could bomb the golf ball (110 mph clubhead speed), but she was a poor wedge player and putter. We were able to get her to break 80 by hitting 5 irons off the tee and 9 irons into the green, whereas she rarely broke 85 with a longer club in her hand from the tee. I was even able to convince her one time to play from 6500 yards instead of 5400 yards, and she shot 78!

So why can these things be problematic? There are three primary problems with these types of phrases or actions:

They serve another master. We are bound by our belief systems, and we live in such a way as to serve those belief systems. If I believe that people are always working an angle, then I will find one regardless of whether there actually is one. I will be distrustful, bitter, and speak poorly of honest people. Put another way, trying to hit it further than your playing partners (or simply being concerned about it) serves the "hitting it further equals lower scores" master. Saying I didn't hit it good (or solid) serves the "I have to hit it perfect" master. Firing at a large number of flags serves the "I don't make mistakes" master. The only master you should be serving is the one that actually causes lower scores.

They distract us from finding the real solution. This is dangerous in that it rarely allows us to look at our rounds objectively. Tour players have extensive stat sheets so that they can look at their rounds with unbiased information. Even with stats, if we continue to serve these other masters, we will look at the stats with rose-colored glasses and not find the real reason for the elevated scores. I'll hear "I couldn't putt" from players to whom I ask, "How long were your putts (for birdie or par)?" Often I'll find that they need to hit it closer, wedge it closer, or make a different decision. Or "I couldn't hit it anywhere" which, in many cases, means players need to take more club or change their strategy; for the club level golfer, it simply means move up a set of tees. Watch out for these distractions or they'll continue to hold you back.

When they work, they reinforce the behavior. Let me illustrate this with an example. If you tell a child "No, don't throw that" and they throw it with no consequence, they will throw it again. Even if you threaten a punishment, if you don't actually punish them, they will throw it again. Then when you finally enforce punishment, it will lack the weight needed to effect change. You think they would stop in the future, but in many cases they don't. Why? The undesired outcome was not initially punished. When you pull off that shot that you can only hit 1 out of 10 or fewer times, it *over-inflates your real ability*. If you play well while angry a few times, it makes you think that playing angry will allow you to perform better every time. (Playing angry is not a sound psychological approach to improved performance).

One last example that many of us have experienced is having a moment over the ball where you feel like you should back off and you don't, but still hit a good shot. This behavior is reinforced, and we are likely to get burned by it in the future, often at the very moment we need something good to happen. So be wary about what you believe, and learn to take a truly objective look at your game as you read through this book.

So how do we get past these harmful traps? Step one is to change your beliefs. Most golfers look at this game and say things like, "It's such a stupid game. "One day I have it, the next day I don't." "How is it possible to do so well for most of my round and screw up those few holes?" "I hate playing with so and so because they hit it everywhere and still beat me—that's so unfair." "His swing is so terrible but. . ." and more! Remember that the universal question, "What did you shoot?" should govern every decision you make.

There are several basic beliefs or principles of golf that are important to keep in mind. There is the ultimate objective with a smaller subset of beliefs. We will refer to these beliefs often, so write them down and commit them to memory:

- The ultimate objective is to shoot the lowest possible score.
- You play golf with your *average* shot.
- There are *two players* in this game:
    - the golf course
    - you
- The golf course is the *defensive* player and the golfer (you) is the *offensive* player.

(Note: In match play format, this *can* change at times.)

Understanding these principles and buying into them 100% will let you see the game and the content within this book with a clear set of lenses.

Your Average Shot

You play golf with your average shot. . .whether you want to or not. Most people are trying to play golf with their best shot, and course architects know this. Let me explain this with something called probability theory.

Probability theory deals with the *analysis* of *random* events in which the events could be one of several *likely* outcomes. The outcome itself is said to be determined by chance. When we set up to hit a shot and decide what we want the ball to do, there is *no guarantee* that the specific shot will happen. We can, however, make a logical guess as to what the ball is *likely* to do and not do. I can predict with 70% (sometimes more) certainty that the outcome could be any one of a number of shots. In a presentation I gave to a group of PGA professionals (and that I do in every one of my private course management lessons), I had two volunteers describe to me their average shot pattern by answering a few questions:

- o Out of 10 shots, how many of them go relatively straight (within a few yards right or left of the target)?
- o How many go to the right? By how many yards?
- o How many go to the left? By how many yards?
- o How many of these 10 go close to the correct distance?
- o How many go short of the correct distance? By how many yards?
- o How many go long of the correct distance? By how many yards?

I then tossed 10 balls out randomly, in this hypothetical educated guess pattern, for each player as though they were aiming directly at the flag. I then ask them to move the pattern of shots as a whole to a spot in which they have the highest percentage chance of shooting the lowest score. (There are a lot more steps to this, but you'll have to come visit me to get the full experience). I then went back in the fairway and had both players hit 10 shots aiming in the selected location (an exercise you will do in Course Two). The magical part about this is that the balls that I tossed randomly are almost in the exact same location as the real shots that they hit. If you've used the DECADE program from BirdieFire, you may be familiar with something similar.[1]

This is where golfers start utilizing the phrase "consistency." They all say they want to be more consistent, but I can already predict what is likely to happen, regardless of their current ability! I've done this dozens upon dozens of times with all ability levels, and everyone is surprised at how accurate this educated guess is to the final outcome.

On the following page, you'll see in the two diagrams the average shot of two different players. The circle around those shots represents about 70% of the shots that each player is likely to hit. Consistency, by definition, is tending to be arbitrarily close to the true value of the parameter estimated as the sample becomes large. What this means is that outcomes are predictable given a large enough sample size. If I asked each player to hit another 20, 30, 40 or more balls, most of those balls will end up in that range. Even the best players in the world have a pattern that varies yet is still predictable. Unfortunately, the average shot that most people pay attention to is the directional component or variance from left to right, but this is only a partial picture, and we must understand that we vary in distance from long to short as well.

---

1 Note to DECADE™ users: What DECADE lacks and Mark Broadie's book *Every Shot Counts* lacks is the human factor. We all have different personalities, risk aversions, short game skill sets, fears, anxieties, and strengths and weaknesses of character. I've coached multiple players who believed that Decade doesn't give them the freedom and flexibility to "be themselves," and they've found the work I've done with them allows them to play to their highest potential. If you are going to use these systems or books you need to understand their shortcomings. Big data can't yet account for these human factors, and this uniqueness is a critical factor in playing your best golf.

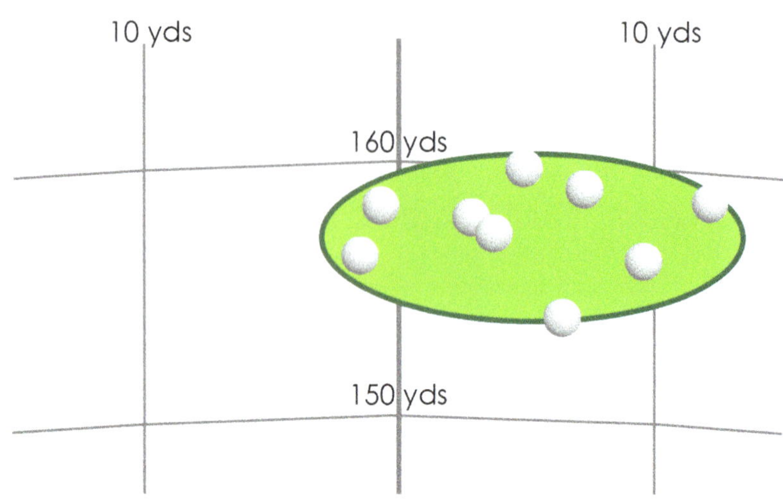
Diagram 1 - Player 1
10 yds
10 yds
160 yds
150 yds

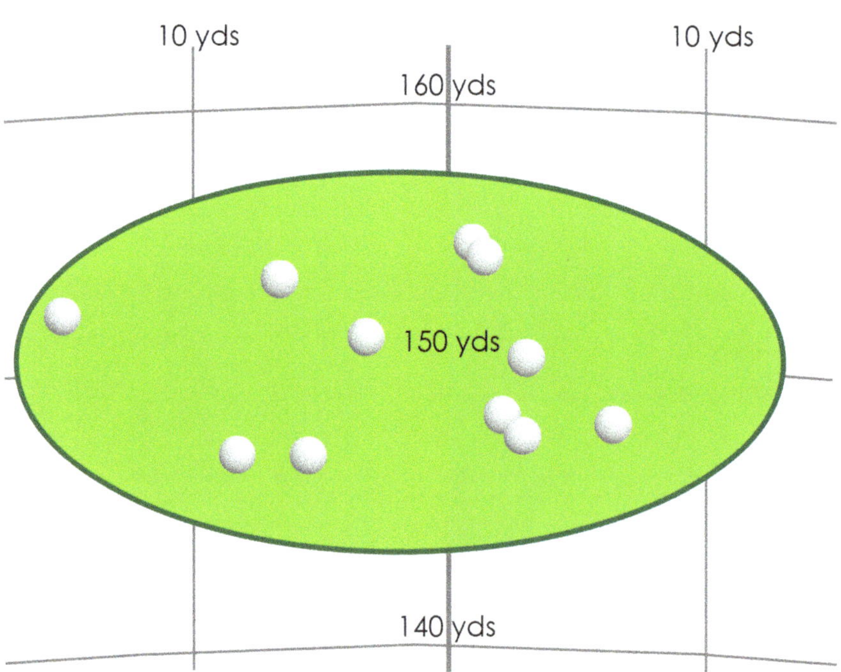
Diagram 2 - Player 2
10 yds
10 yds
160 yds
150 yds
140 yds

In Mark Broadie's book, *Every Shot Counts*, he performs simulations on a computer of golfers of various ability levels accounting for the "shot pattern of a typical 100 (or 80) golfer." He is 100% correct to consider their average shots, not just a single ideal shot. What he misses in his analysis, though, is that humans are not machines. We do not make decisions solely on hard data. Data is awesome and helpful, but following computer simulations doesn't always equate to a lower score, even for the best players in the world. Our emotions or "instincts" can be crucial determinants to the outcome of a given hole or tournament. There have been countless tournaments both at the amateur and tour level where players have attempted shots that the data would not support but led to a successful victory. Take Phil Mickelson's famous 6-iron on the Par 5 13th at the 2010 Masters from the pine straw as an example. He hit it to 10 feet guaranteeing him birdie and an opportunity at eagle at a crucial point in the tournament.

One of my college players, Austin, needed an eagle on the final hole in order for the team to win the conference championship in 2019. He tried to cut off the dogleg on the par 5 and hit it over an adjacent hole. He was left with 197 yards and could either punch out to the fairway or hit a rope hook that started out of bounds and hooked back in play. He took on the risk, hit the ball to 12 feet, and sank the putt for eagle to win the conference championship. The reason we don't see these or similar examples supporting sound course management strategy is that it doesn't fit the "big data" profile. They are shots with low probabilities, but some part of us just knows that we'll pull it off. What I hope to show you, and to help you understand in your own game, is when to follow the data and when to follow your gut. If you do both, you can play spectacular golf!

Two Players

Jack Nicklaus said, "Success depends almost entirely on how effectively you manage the game's two ultimate adversaries: the golf course and yourself."

No truer words are spoken about the game of golf. While we play golf with other people, the illusion is that we are playing *against* one another. This may be further illumined by the definition of Game Theory: The branch of mathematics concerned with the analysis of strategies for dealing with competitive situations where the outcome of a participant's course of action depends critically on the actions of other participants.

There are several important pieces of that definition, but the operative word is *critically*. What my playing partner or opponent does on a given shot or hole has no effect of any significance as to what I do on a given shot or hole. While we are playing together, it may appear that one person is "beating" another or has "bested" another. The decisions and shots that you hit should have no effect on those that I make. From the highest to the lowest levels of golf, every person has a unique set of skills, experiences, fears, and behaviors that are unique to them. While they play the same course (with exceptions for changes in weather/conditions over the course of a day), they must fit their set of characteristics to the layout before them that produces for them the lowest possible score in the highest number of circumstances. The nature of the etiquette and rules of the game don't allow us to act defensively toward another player: There are no stymies, no shouting, no pushing, blocking, or defending of shots or swings. You execute your strategy and swing, and your opponents execute theirs. Nothing more than that, and nothing less.

Course = Defense / You = Offense

The golf course and you have very specific roles and they cannot (and should not) change! The golf course is exclusively the defensive player and the golfer the offensive player. Why? If we simply look at the singular goal or purpose of the offensive and defensive players in any sport, you'll find that the purpose of the defense is to *prevent scoring* and that of the offense is *to score*. Some of you may be asking one of two questions: "What about the situation in which the green slope moves a ball toward the hole?" or "What of a player aiming away from a pin or hitting an iron off the tee in order to play defensively?"

Let's steer this argument away from golf to another sport, basketball. Consider two different defensive strategies: man-to-man and zone. These two strategies serve to prevent the offense of the opposing team from scoring. They are trying to match the best defense to the offense they are playing. While shifting to a zone defense may prevent fast drives to the basket or to make an exceptional offensive player less effective, it does not entirely prevent them from scoring. It simply forces the offense to use other means to score, such as making more outside shots or forcing other players to shoot instead of the star player. While both the man-to-man and zone defenses prevent certain things from happening, they open up the possibility of different ways of scoring by the offense.

Conversely, when an offense chooses to keep driving to the basket in order to make a shorter shot or draw fouls, they could be said to be playing defensively especially when they have a large lead. You wouldn't say they are playing defensively; however, you would say they are choosing a different offensive strategy. They are still trying to *score*, not keep themselves from scoring. I really don't like it when golfers or coaches use phrases like "play defensively" on this hole or shot. It may sound like semantics, but words have powerful implications for behavior and emotion. People who choose to play "defensively" begin to make tentative, unconfident, and poor swings. They also begin to feel excessive nerves, fear, or begin to believe they aren't very good. When you choose to layup, play away from a flag, or hit a shorter club off the tee, it is vital that you *know* that those are *offensive* tactics, though they may be more conservative in nature.

As the offensive player, it's essential that you know yourself well. You need to know your skill set intimately in every area—from the putter to the driver, the particular style of golf courses and holes you play well, your particular fears, your personality, and your stat profile. Most players have a general idea, but few have a deep understanding of what they are capable of doing. Even when armed with this information, you may not make the best decisions. The exercise at the end of this course will help you become more acquainted with yourself.

FOR ADVANCED PLAYERS

For those who are advanced, I watch you struggle in two ways because certain principles are missing:

You don't take a truly objective look at your rounds. You rationalize your decisions based on what you "thought" you should do or be able to do. This often sounds like "I got a bad break," "If I had just made those two putts I lipped out," "I just don't play this course well," etc.

And it affects your mental game in that you struggle with confidence or fire at most or all of the flags because you're a great ball striker. This often looks like inward and outward expressions of disappointment or frustration, taking aggressive lines, having a high percentage of short-sided shots (anything over 20% of your up and down attempts that come from short sided or difficult situations is far too many), or a number of would-be great rounds that are ruined by a single, or multiple, bad holes.

So what do you do about it? (I'll elaborate on the mental game in the upcoming courses and more fully in the final course.) Ask yourself this fundamental question: Is this a *must* situation or a *want* situation? You'll keep your instincts intact, but begin to eliminate the detrimental errors that seemingly compound one another.

The Champions Takeaways

- "What did you shoot?" must govern every decision you make.
- What you believe *affects* your behavior, and your behaviors *reflect* what you believe.
- Behaviors that go against the universal question are problematic as they serve another master; they keep you from finding the best solution, and when they work, they can reinforce damaging behavior.

- You play golf with your *average shot.*
- There are two players in the game: the golf course and you. You are the *offensive player* and the course is the *defensive player.*
- Golf is a game of chance, but the outcome is *predictable.*

For Advanced Players

- Remember to ask: Is this a *must* situation or a *want* situation?

Exercise #1: Get to Know Y-O-U!

Before you get into any of the assignments, keep in mind that they are designed to help you LEARN how to play your best golf. Some of the exercises may cause you to play *worse* in certain circumstances, but they are there to help you learn what's best *for you.*

This is a two-part exercise designed to help you know yourself better. Complete each part *fully* and *in order* before moving on to Course Two. (The tables are on the following pages.)

Part 1: Complete Table 1 as accurately as you can. I have filled in some example content to guide you. This table will allow you to take a closer look at the shots you are capable of hitting and help you understand your likely misses.

Part 1b (optional): If you have access to a Trackman or Flightscope, complete a full club-gapping (you may need to break it into two days) with 10 shots on every club in your bag except your putter. Find a local golf professional who can do a club gapping for you. Fill in the content for this portion on Table #2 once you have this data.

Part 1c: Play 18-36 holes with the actual numbers from Trackman. If you don't have access to this technology and have a handicap more than 0, add one club to every approach shot you hit *except to a back pin or with a partial wedge shot.*

Part 2: Hard data. I love stats, they tell us a lot about your game. If you already track stats, GREAT! If not, consider downloading one and commit to using it on every round.

Table 1 - Your Shot Pattern

	Your Estimated Shot Pattern			
Club	Carry Distance	% Relatively Straight	% Left	% Right
60 56				
52				
PW				
9 Iron	161	6	3	1
8 Iron				
7 Iron				
6 Iron				
5 Iron				
4 Iron (hyb)				
3 Iron (hyb)				
2 Iron (hyb)				
7 wood				
5 wood				
3 wood				
Driver				

Basic Stats (estimate if unknown)				
HDCP (avg. score)	GIR	FIR	U/D%	Putts/Round
3.2	8	10	55%	29

Table 2 - Trackman Shot Pattern

Club	Carry Distance	% Relatively Straight	% Left	% Right	Standard Deviation Direction	% Long	% Short	Standard Deviation Distance
60								
56								
52								
PW								
9 Iron								
8 Iron								
7 Iron								
6 Iron								
5 Iron								
4 Iron (hyb)								
3 Iron (hyb)								
2 Iron (hyb)								
7 wood								
5 wood								
3 wood								
Driver								

It is much too large a subject to go into question of the placing of hazards, but I would like to emphasize a fundamental principle. It is that, as already pointed out, no hazard is unfair wherever it is placed. A hazard placed in the exact position where a player would naturally go is frequently the most interesting situation, as then a special effort is needed to go over or avoid it.

— Alistair Mackenzie

COURSE TWO: UNDERSTANDING THE ARCHITECT

LET'S FACE IT, GOLF COURSE ARCHITECTS HAVE THE UPPER HAND. They know you better than you know yourself. The even crazier part is they know all of you regardless of your ability, experience, or personality. They know the likely places you'll miss, what scares you, what you like and dislike, and they know what you will decide before you do. Architects know their designs insanely well—the subtle slopes on the green; the subtle shapes of a hole, green, or teeing ground; how one hole is likely to affect the next few; little visual tricks meant to fool you; how a hole will play in various weather conditions, and more. This section helps shed light on their strategies so that you can have a leg up on your competition and on the architect.

I want to start by having you build a course map. If you happen to play at a golf course that has a yardage book, then you may use that to your advantage, but you will still need to complete the exercises in this section. You will see the best players in the world use a yardage book on almost every shot, and some of the tour caddy yardage books will make your head spin with the amount of information they provide. So why do they have yardage books, and why should you have one? Let's take a look at three important elements of maps in general:

- o Maps tell us *what.*
- o Maps provide *important information.*
- o Maps create *familiarity* and help us *understand* our surroundings.

There are many kinds of maps from various fields of study; all serve to provide these same three important pieces of information. With advances in modern technology and programs like Google Earth, Blue Golf, and Google Maps, you can build a map of virtually any landscape or cityscape you choose and navigate to the nearest foot.

First, a golf course map tells us some basic (and sometimes detailed) information about *what* we are looking at. As you build and review your map, you can add additional elements to it.

Second, maps also provide *important information* relevant to the purpose which they serve. For instance, if you are traveling to a state park, you would want to know where the ranger office, trailheads, and bathrooms are located. You may also want to know how long each trail is and have a compass to guide you should you get lost or need to alert emergency personnel.

Lastly, maps help us *become familiar* with the area we are navigating. This allows us to minimize mistakes, anxiety, and potential costs. A golf course superintendent's map of the course would look very different from the golfer's in that it would likely include locations of sprinkler heads, underground irrigation pipes, and electrical wiring. The golfer's would include the lay of the course, hole locations, and the prevailing winds. In *The*

Five Elements of Effective Thinking, Starbird and Burger note, "Whenever you 'see' an issue or 'understand' a concept, be conscious of the lens through which you're viewing the subject. You should assume you are introducing bias. The challenge remains to identify and let go of that bias or the assumptions you bring, and actively work to see and understand the subject anew." As you determine what to add to your yardage book, look for ways to include information that helps you understand more fully what is in front of you. This information should have three elements:

- It should be relevant to you.
- It should be accurate.
- There should be the right amount.

Relevant information means information that is important for *you* to have—yardages, landing areas, key landmarks, hazards, compass, notes on visual tricks, slopes, and likely pin locations are examples of relevant information. Someone who carries the ball 290 yards off the tee and hits it really straight may not include carry distances over a bunker that only requires a 220-yard carry from the tee. Someone who hits it just as far, but can be wild with the driver, may want to know this information so they can select an appropriate alternative club that guarantees they will carry that hazard.

Relevant information should also match your skill level and personality. If you are a 15+ handicap, you may not be looking for specific green information—amount of slope, flattest part of the fairway, best angle to approach a pin, etc.—as you may not yet have the skill set for which that information would be helpful to you. And if you have an artistic, "feel-oriented" brain, you may only need basic information about the course—places you like to aim, carry distances of various objects, likely pin placements—but not specific numbers on the green slopes. There is no "right" answer, but there are likely some wrong answers.

The information you put on your course map must also be accurate. The hole shape, places you aim, compass angle, and carry distances must be correct. If you rely on bad information, you're likely to end up in bad places with subsequent disappointment and frustration. Slope on range finders help players add or subtract yardage based on the elevation changes. However, as the elevation gets more severe, it may or may not play that exact yardage uphill or downhill.

What your ball flight does has an impact on the amount of change in yardage, so don't be afraid to hit a few extra shots in your practice rounds in these scenarios to make sure the information is correct. If you mark likely pin locations, make sure you have the exact yardage from the front and sides of the green and carry distances over certain parts of the green, if applicable for you. If you use yardages that are approximations or are off by a few yards, you're missing opportunities to shoot lower scores. (If you are off by just three yards, that's nearly 10 feet; the best players in the world make less than 50% of their putts from 10 feet, and the percentage drops substantially from there.)

Case Study: Brent, Handicap +1.0

Brent joined my course management class in the fall of 2018 as a mid-am tournament golfer looking to find extra strokes on his golf game, particularly in his tournament play.

He is a wonderful ball striker averaging around 12.5 greens in regulation and hitting over 75% of his fairways. Brett's biggest problem was that he played with vague approximations. I discovered that he almost never played to a specific yardage. Even though he had a rangefinder, he would shoot the yardage and hit it "about" 150 instead of 154 or 147, especially on his short irons and wedges. Brett didn't know specific carry yardages or utilize a yardage book when he played. He would make pars and occasionally some "silly" bogeys with these clubs. This led him to be more aggressive on his long-irons and sometimes take more aggressive lines off the tee on holes with narrow fairways in an effort to "get back" the strokes he believed he was losing on those holes. Within five weeks of starting the class, I had Brett's handicap trending at a +3.2! He had fired multiple rounds of 66 or better, improved his proximity to the hole, and had his confidence soaring through the roof.

So how did I solve Brett's dilemma? The first thing I did with Brett was to make sure he tried to hit to a specific yardage while favoring a specific side of the hole. I had him taking more aggressive lines with his short clubs and more conservative lines with his longer clubs. He was a great ball striker so I helped him to identify specific locations to hit the ball. He used to simply step up and just swing with a feel that he thought would work.

I love "feel" players like Brett who have high levels of skill because a little precision in their decision making can lead to massive improvements in their scoring. I have also found that many of these players are seeking sports psychology help when they don't really need it, they just need a new way of looking at the game. Brett was a guy who already had good course management skills. I meet a lot of Bretts who believe deeply they should be shooting lower scores, but they can't identify why. They wrongly assume that they "know how to play" and therefore can't ever truly identify the reasons for their poor performance. The message is this: Use your yardage book to provide you with the information you need, don't be general. Be careful, be accurate.

The third element is probably the hardest of all. The *right amount* of information. This is where my classes at our academy are very helpful. We review the yardage books as a group and help each other identify what is too much and what is not enough. The most helpful analogy I can provide is that of Goldilocks and the Three Bears: too much, not enough, just right.[1]

I often get students asking for more specifics when it comes to building their yardage books. Because of the uniqueness of each, I could write a whole book as to what's acceptable for which player, which scenario, which course and more. Understand that maps need three basic pieces of information: relevance, accuracy, and the right amount of it. In order to satisfy inquiring minds, I'll leave you with a few final guidelines and three questions that you can ask yourself when you're building these maps.

1Green Complexes. The Green should have the *most detail* of any of your drawings. Given that the ball will end up here, that 40% of your shots come from putting alone, another 25% come from wedges onto the green, and that your approach shots which account for 15% of all the shots you'll hit are going to try to land on or near the green, it's important that you get key information on the green complex. *That's 80% of your shots!* It should be accurately drawn in both distance and direction with carry distances precisely measured to certain features like tiers, slopes, or clearances over hazards. There are several programs out there that allow you to gather this information ahead of time so there shouldn't be a reason for you not to have this!

Guidelines

You should be able to build your yardage book during the course of play. If you're taking 5+ hours to complete it, you've missed the point

Use technology to your advantage. Flag Hunting, Google Earth and BlueGolf allow you to measure and draw things accurately ahead of time.

I recommend you use Go To Caddie yardage books if you want to build it by hand or Flag Hunting if you want to build it digitally. If you are a collegiate player, I would push your coaches to get you setup with yardage books from a company called Strackaline. For PGA professionals, if your goal is to grow the game, then you should have your courses professionally mapped as is done for the PGA Tour. (You don't need the colorful books with the specifics on how to play the hole; if you want that, use the digital platforms on your website.) The technology exists and the game is becoming one governed by big data. Spend the money, and the game will return the thanks. Let's stay ahead of the global trends, not behind!

Three questions:

- What do I *see?*
- What do I *need?*
- What information could *help* me?

These three questions will help give some structure to your yardage book and help remove any bias you may bring to the table when building it. When you ask the question "What do I see?," you simply want to *acknowledge* what's there. This includes the broad layout of the hole, down to the smallest details. Knowing what you *need* is a matter of determining appropriate information that you'll likely use at some point in time. This may be different than the information that could help you. Information that could *help* you might include the slope on the green that moves the ball toward the hole. You don't necessarily *need* this information, but it could be helpful to you in the right circumstance.

Utilize this information to build your yardage book, and learn to use your yardage book every time you play. The exercise at the end of this section asks you to build a yardage book for your home course and includes a second section that will be necessary for you to become elite in course management. Just as making a swing change requires repetition to become a habit, so does using your map. Use it in practice so that you're comfortable when you play in tournaments. You'll shoot lower scores more often! I'll show you how to use these yardage books in the remaining sections of this book.

FOR ADVANCED PLAYERS

If you are a collegiate, amateur, mid-amateur, or tour level golfer, then you might already be using yardage books. You might even be someone whose yardage book looks like a mathematics textbook. If you are using one, I want you to get in the habit of building it before you play, using it while you play, and reviewing it after you play. Consider likely scenarios such as with prevailing winds, how you might play it differently on a less than or better than average day, changes in tournament pins or tee locations, or changes in course conditions due to weather. These factors can change the information you might include on your yardage book. You could also ask other "better" players how they plan to play the course. I even suggest that you ride or walk the course backwards to get a more informed perspective on how the hole is designed to be played (more on this in subsequent courses). There's no excuse for you not to do everything in your power to be prepared!

If you do not currently use a yardage book, get in the habit of using one. I find it interesting when elite players who rarely use yardage books decide to use one in a big tournament. There are two problems with this: First, you don't have a clue what to pay attention to and what to ignore. It becomes something you do just because you see other people doing it. In most cases, these players include irrelevant and excessive information that they misuse because they haven't made it part of their routines. Second, because you are not in the habit of using a yardage book, your performance is questionable. I've seen players use one for just these events and play better, but I've seen far more finally use a yardage book but play worse because they are out of their comfort zone. I often hear "I was just overthinking." Of course, you were! You're trying to process information that you rarely consider. Or you obsess about the information, trying to find a way to make up the strokes you've lost in order to get to a specific score. Start using a yardage book the majority of time you play so that it becomes natural for you to utilize the detailed information.

The Champions Takeaways

- The course architects have the upper hand. It's *their* course and they often know *you* better than you do.

- o A yardage book needs to have three types of information:
  - o Relevant, accurate, and the right amount
- o When creating your yardage book, identify three things:
  - o What you see, what you need, and what information can help you

FOR ADVANCED PLAYERS

- o Little details can make a big difference. If you're not using a yardage book, start NOW, and use it daily!

EXERCISE #2: KNOW THE COURSE, TEST YOUR SKILLS

Part 1: *Build a Map* for your home course utilizing the guidelines presented in the course. Review it after you design it before beginning to play with it. If you already have one, take some time to review it and go in and make some edits. (If you don't edit or change anything, then you likely haven't learned anything!) I will teach you how to use it in future sections.

Part 2: *Your Average Shot.* Select three different *approach* shots (or tee shot on a par 3) on your home course of varying distances and hole designs. Play from the fairway and use a short iron, mid-iron, and long-iron or hybrid.

Select a place to aim, both in distance and direction, for the given shot. For example: three yards short and five yards right of the flag.

Hit 10 balls using your full routine at the exact same target. *Use the same target on every shot.* Use a friend or alignment aid to ensure you're doing this exercise in a precise manner.

Green Diagrams

Example 1

Example 2

Finish out all 10 balls. Record the results on Table #3. The results will be discussed in Course Three: Have a Plan.

You may also use the hole/green maps provided by Go To Caddie to mark where your 10 approach shots finished up.

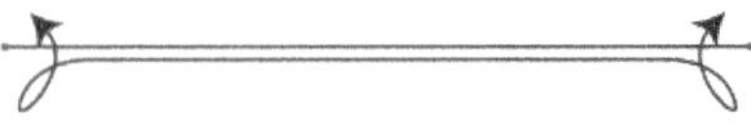

Table 3 - Your Average Shot

Hole:		Yardage:		Pin Location:	
Club	Green Hit (Y/N)	Prox. to Hole (ft)	Putts	U/D (Y/N)	Score
1					
2					
3					
4					
5					
6					
7					
8					
9					
10					
Totals					
Averages					

Note: Assume you are going for the green in regulation, the shot you are hitting would, therefore, be for eagle (1st shot on a par 3, 2nd shot on a par 4, 3rd shot on a par 5).

Diagram 3, Course 2

Hole ______ Par ______ Yardage ______

Paces: Front to Back ______

Slope Direction ______ Side to Side ______

Green Diagram

False Front/Flat Front

Notes:

Example of a green grid from a Go To Caddie yardage book.

. . .I stress three dimensions when I talk about strategy: You have to understand your personal capabilities, you have to understand the trouble spots on the course, and you have to play every shot with the next shot in mind.

—Tom Watson

COURSE THREE: Have a Plan

IF YOU'VE EVER TRAVELED FOR VACATION, YOU'VE PROBABLY CREATED A PLAN FOR YOUR TRIP. Even you free-spirited types have some idea where you're going, what you're going to do, how you plan to get there, or how long you will be gone. We make plans for our education, plans for our careers, plans for our finances, plans for our travels, plans for our families, and we talk about plans that our favorite sports teams and athletes should employ in order to be successful, but we don't make plans for when we play golf! Those who are playing for pure leisure I can understand, but I'm amazed at how many give little, no, or poor thought to how they plan to play the course. Even board game junkies have plans and strategies that they'll use in order to give themselves the best chance of winning.

When we decide to go on a vacation, we first take time to decide on our destination. We can't build a trip without this; your golf game is the same. In order to construct a plan for the golf course, we must first look at where the ball will come to rest. In fact, the *only thing* that matters about *any* given shot is *where it ends up!* None of the following things matter:

- o How *solid* you hit it
- o How *perfectly* you hit it
- o How *focused* you were
- o How *far* you hit it
- o What *club* you hit or
- o How *it got there*

The only thing that matters is that it got "there," wherever that might be. When it goes where we want, we say things like, "Did you see the shot I hit on 11?! It was incredible!" When it goes better than we wanted, we say things like, "Wow, that was lucky!" When it goes where we didn't want, we often say things like, "I got such a bad break" or "Those putts should've gone in!"

In reality, all of it is "luck," a game of chance over which you have a certain amount of influence but not absolute control. Remember the rules of probability theory: You can't guarantee a specific outcome, but it is likely to be any one of a number of possibilities with the precise outcome being determined by chance. That's why Tom Watson mentions you have to understand your personal capabilities. We all have a different "chance" of hitting a good shot or the shot we desire. I tell all my students that their golf swing—from their putting to their driving—has a unique percentage chance of executing a shot. They come to me as an instructor to increase that number. Failure to understand this deeply leads to loads of bad decision making and the corresponding frustration or disappointment.

Let's take a few minutes to review the 10-shot exercise you completed in Exercise #2: Part 2. You'll notice that not all 10 shots ended up exactly where you wanted them. Some may have been pretty close, some better, and some worse. This is exactly why I talk about the principle of probability theory. This is your source of success and enjoyment of the game.

Take time to answer the following questions about the exercise (do not respond with swing/technique changes):

- o What did you like that happened?
- o What didn't you like?
- o What was the general pattern of your shots?
- o What could or would you have changed about the target you selected in order to improve your *average* score? To make more birdies or less bogeys/doubles?

Whether or not you liked the outcome of the exercise is of little value. It's what you've learned from the exercise that really matters. The shots that you hit are all reasonable and likely outcomes, even if you were having a "bad day!" *Take a moment to let that soak that in.* Throughout the rest of this book, your short and long term performance and your enjoyment of the game rely on the principles that the 10-shot exercise teaches. *If you don't get anything else from this book, get this section.* These principles are:

- o There is one universal question: What did you shoot?
- o We all play golf with our average shot.
- o The specific outcome of this is determined by chance with results that are largely predictable.
- o Where the ball ends up is the only thing that matters in shooting your lowest score.

This is why I'm dumbfounded when players, especially good players (<10 handicap), tell me they want to be more consistent. They are *already* consistent in their behaviors, and the outcomes can be predicted. What they really want is more certainty about what will happen, which is referred to in the science world as "precision"—groupings are more closely matched to one another. I'll share an example that happened with some of my juniors who said they wanted to be "more consistent."

Case Study: Ben and Jerry

Take a look at the shot patterns in the following images: Player A (Ben) and Player B (Jerry).

- o Which player would you say is more consistent?
- o Which player would you say is more aggressive?
- o Which player would you rather have on your four-ball team or in your scramble?
- o Who is the better player?

. . .

The truth is they are the exact same player with the exact same shot pattern!

At first glance it appears that the dispersion pattern of player B is better than that of player A. Keep this in mind, though, the slopes around the green determine the final resting place of the ball. I asked this student what club he would hit and how far he would hit it. I added eight yards to his yardage and he took one additional club and hit a knock down. The results shown for Player B (Jerry) were the actual shots he hit. The results for Player A (also Jerry) were found by taking the landing spot of

Diagram 4

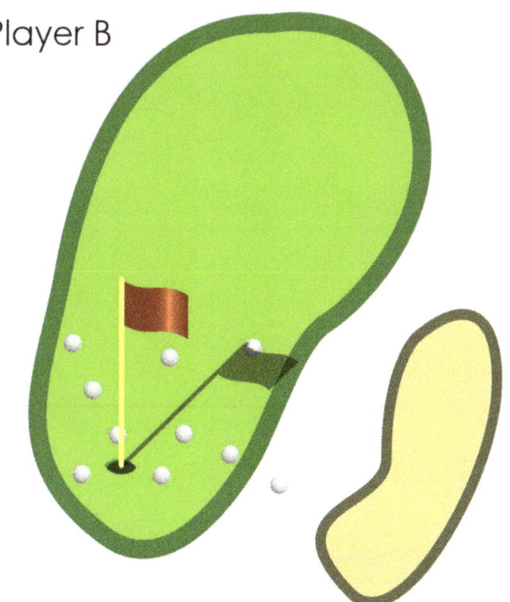

Whom would you rather have on your scramble team?

Player A's balls and walking straight back eight yards toward where he played from and dropping those balls from shoulder height.

The final resting place of those balls was determined by the slopes around the green. Every ball that got dropped short of the green rolled back away from the hole because the slope short of the green is fairly severe, as you can see below.

Diagram with Slopes

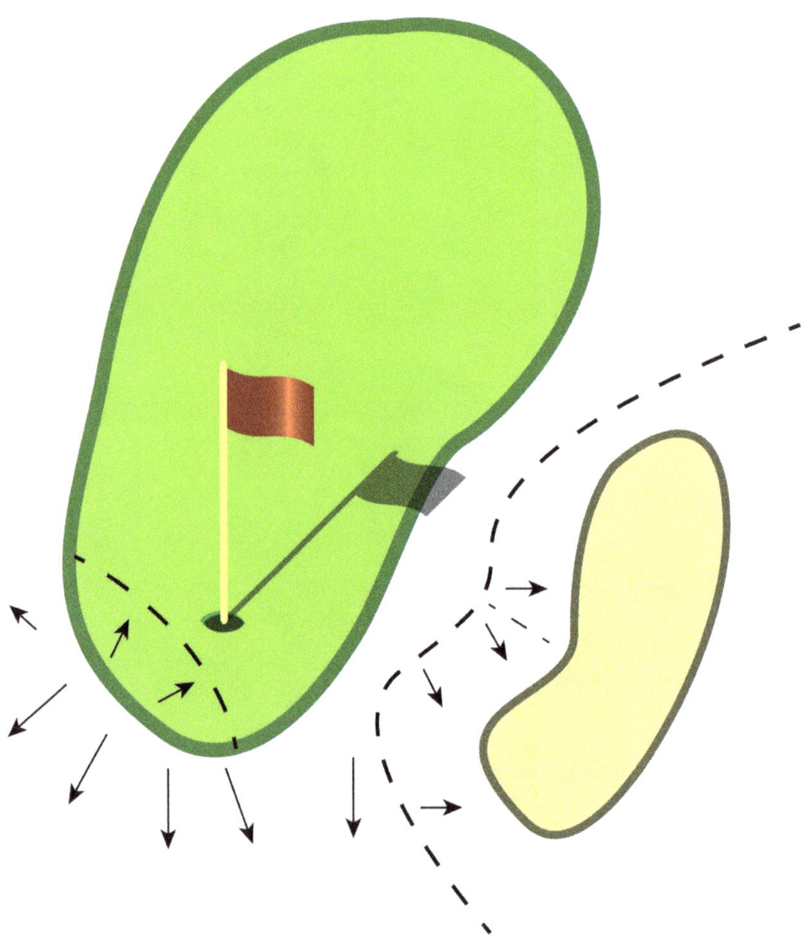

I then had Jerry finish these balls out, as well. The results of this exercise are shown in the chart below.

Shot Pattern Scores

Player A Shot Pattern Score	Player B Shot Pattern Score	
4	3	
4	4	
5	3	
4	4	
4	4	
5	4	
4	4	
5	4	
5	4	
4	4	
4.4	3.8	Stroke Average Played 10 Times
+0.4	-0.2	Relation to Par on Average
0.6		Average Differential

I then proceeded to show him the above chart with the final score once all the balls were finished out. What you will see is a dramatic improvement in *average* score. If you select any one score from the diagram from either shot selection, sometimes they tie, but on the average shot, selection B beats shot selection A. In some cases, the results are more dramatic and sometimes less dramatic than this, and in some cases the worse average beats the better average *on a single attempt*. Let's go one step further: If I take this average and spread it out over the course of 18 holes, that's an improvement of 10.8 strokes! Some holes are less than this so let's cut it in half and make it 5.4 strokes per round, which is a realistic number for this young man to improve, if he can learn to make decisions like this. Further still, even if it's not that good and we make only 30% of the 10.8, that's 3.25 strokes per round, and we haven't even addressed the tee shot yet!

When the students who have completed my class or been on the golf course with me make decisions like this, their average improvement is *more than 3.25 strokes*. Even for an accomplished player like Brent from Course Two, we saw an improvement of 2.2 strokes. I've had players improve more than 5 strokes on strategy alone (one young man at a local high school improved over 9 strokes in four weeks). These numbers are incredible! While that may not sound like a lot of strokes on the average, imagine how much happier you would be if your handicap went from 7 to 3.75, a 12 to an 8.5, or an 18 or 20 to a 15?! Here's the crazy thing though, a player like Brent may only need one or two strokes per round to finish in the top 10 or win the tournament (especially a three- or four-day tournament).

My passion is helping players and programs shoot lower scores and enjoy the game at a higher level. I was so excited to work with Miles College in Birmingham midway through their 2018 fall season in 2018. I did the 10-shot exercise with them with a little additional content over the course of two afternoons. I remember two of the guys on the team, who were the first to hit 10 shots at the location we decided on, saying after they completed the exercise, "I thought he was out of his mind, but he was dead on with that exercise!"

We repeated this in several other circumstances discussing some other pre-shot thought routines with the same improved outcome every time. The team won their next two events! The first two guys who did the exercise had their personal best collegiate tournaments, and one of them won an event as an individual. I'll go as far as to say that high school and college programs that commit to play this way could see as much as an 8 to 10 stroke improvement *per tournament round*! This would take many teams from the middle to top in their conference and vying or competing for national championship titles. Just like any lesson in life, it's important to be reminded of the things we've learned in the past in order to prevent making the same mistakes over and over.

The most important thing I want you to understand from this section is the principle of playing with your average shot. For those who completed the Trackman or Flightscope portion from Course One, you'll notice I asked for your standard deviation in distance and direction. What this really tells you is that you can expect your shots to finish within this distance (long, short, left, right) approximately 70% of the time. You will, on occasion, have shots that finish outside of this, but the likelihood is much lower.[1]

You don't need to memorize your standard deviation or the exact pattern of shots you'll hit. I just want you to understand that you have a pattern, and this is what it is likely to be. In the days leading up to an event, you could get this information again to get a better idea of how you're really hitting the ball. This is the biggest advantage to having this technology at your disposal. On several occasions, Jordan Spieth has been known to use the

---

1 If you are making poor decisions and have a lot of tension, nerves, or anxiety about a particular miss, then you either don't believe this or you are most likely selecting a shot that it is not probable to end up in a favorable position (the ball is highly likely to end up in trouble). This will cause you to execute that other 30% more often as those tensions interrupt the execution of a confident swing! This is why the mental game is the last section in my book!

Trackman to determine how much the wind will affect the ball (right, left, headwind, tailwind). He's focused on *where the ball ends up*. As we work through the remainder of this book, you'll be able to develop your own instincts and patterns of thought that will help you arrive at optimal solutions. So how do you decide what exactly to do on a given shot?

Deciding your precise course of action is a mix of what is factually true about you and what makes you comfortable. These two things can be in line with one another or create friction with one another. It's awesome when they align, but deciding which one should win out or influence the other is a matter of experience and self-reflection. Consider how far on average you hit the ball, how much and how often left or right you hit it, and how well you can actually execute your desired shot. This will often lead you to a more comfortable shot selection, though not always. When I talk about comfortable, I'm referring to what shot selection makes you feel the *most* confident and simply "feels the best" or "fits your eye." Consider both of these when you build your strategy in Exercise 3 (page 47).

For Advanced Players

It's time to determine if you're an aggressive or a conservative personality. First, *I don't believe there are "right" or "wrong" decisions.* There is only *risk and reward*. Assuming you have the same skill set, you *cannot* play the same way. If you play too far away from your given personality, you are likely to underperform. I can't reinforce this enough. This is where I break the most heavily away from the other books and programs that are out there. Players that play away from this make unconfident, frustrated, or distracted swings. Remember what I mentioned above about the *other 30%*? We are more likely to make those happen if we play away from our natural personalities. Are aggressive personalities likely to make bogies or some doubles? Absolutely. But they are also likely to make a lot of birdies. Are conservative personalities likely to not make enough birdies? Absolutely. But they are also likely to make very few mistakes. If you don't know yourself very well, I suggest you take the Mental Golf Workshop profiling test. It will help illuminate your personality strengths.

The other things to understand are: How good is my short game? How good am I from the bunker? deep rough? short sided? bump and runs? high flop shots? 20, 30, 40 or 50 yard shots? uneven lies greenside?, etc. If you are a great ball striker with an aggressive personality, but you are a poor wedge player, then you may have to make more conservative decisions that reduce your risk of having to fight for an up and down. This is one of the reasons college programs fight so hard for players to develop fantastic short games. It opens up the option of more aggressive lines for more birdie opportunities, while reducing the risk of bogies, doubles, or worse. If you have a mediocre short game, I'm sorry, but your options are limited.

Case Study: Elaine, Elite College Golfer

When Elaine and I worked together she became a world class ball striker but lacked the skills in her wedge play to take advantage of some of the shorter holes like par 5s that she might be able to reach in two, or par 4s that she could drive the green or get close. Where she struggled was from 20 to 60 yards. I knew if she was ever going to be great, we had to do two things: First, she had to avoid this distance range altogether. She won two events playing like this before this area of her game ever got better. Second, she had to get better at shots from this distance. Then she would have the freedom to take advantage of her great ball-striking. As this area of her game improved, she went on to win three more events and advance to the NCAA DII National Championship and became an All-American finishing inside the top 15!

The other thing you must do: Track your statistics! Get a detailed program that allows you to get to know your game intimately. Stop guessing about what you think you can do or what you think you should be able to do. Know what you can actually do and make decisions that simultaneously improve your scores and increase your confidence. I am baffled when elite players don't track this information or when they rely on a very watered-down version of their stats to guide them. If you want to beat the best, then you *need to know* what you can really do. Keep in mind that the guys and girls on the PGA and LPGA tours have statistics sheets that are pages long, and they have people who will analyze it for them. If you ever dream of competing against those types of players or the top players in your state or region, then you better get in the habit of tracking this data. It's foolish to think it's not necessary.

THE CHAMPIONS TAKEAWAYS

- There are only four things that matter:
    - What did you shoot?

    - o You play golf with your average shot
    - o The outcome of your shots are determined by chance
    - o Where the ball ends up is the only thing that matters in determining your final score.
- o Know yourself well.
- o The goal is to improve your average score, not just make one hole, round, or shot better.

For Advanced Players

- o Track your stats in detail.
- o Know your skill set inside out.
- o Know your personality and play close to it.

Exercise #3: Develop Your Plan

It's time for you to begin learning how to use your yardage book. The first step is setting a plan for every hole and the likely shots you'll face. I've provided some examples to help you get started. (See pages 49 and 50.)

Part 1: Build a plan. Select a target and club for each tee shot and each approach shot to several likely pin placements, including advancements on par 5s (both distance and direction). I like to have players label the likely hole locations with a capital letter (A, B, C, etc.) and where they want the ball to end up with a lowercase letter (a, b, c, etc.). This will help guide your distance and target selection.

Part 2: Play to this plan exactly for 18 to 36 holes. Do not veer from the plan one bit. Even if you begin to feel like the decision you've made isn't the best in the moment, follow it precisely so as to illuminate important principles. You might find it's still a good decision. Make notes about what worked well and what you might consider changing.

Green Diagram

Hole 7 Par 4 Yardage 447

Paces: Front to Back 33

Slope Direction —— Side to Side ——

Green Diagram

N
D
d
c
C
b
B
a
A

False Front/Flat Front

Notes:

Balls run off back of green to collection area.

Green Diagram

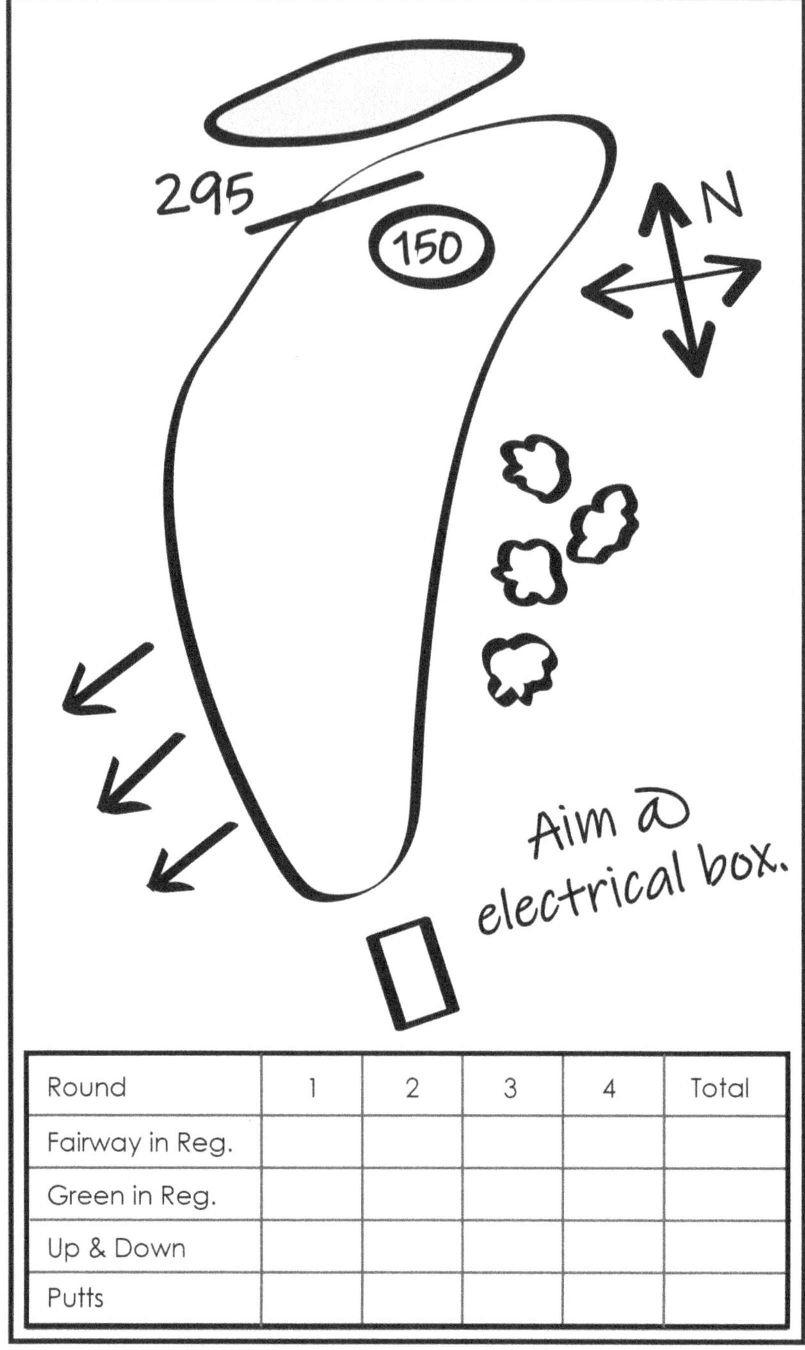

Round	1	2	3	4	Total
Fairway in Reg.					
Green in Reg.					
Up & Down					
Putts					

Think management. You want to always get your ball into 'the mayor's office,' the sweet spot on the fairway where you can attack the pins. Simple as that!

—George Lucas, Former Caddie

COURSE FOUR: Revising Your Plan

In the world of writing, art, music, and even architecture, drafts are an integral part of the process to bring a work to completion. Rarely, if ever, is a great piece of work completed in the first or second draft. Even this book and the corresponding classes on site have gone through multiple drafts to arrive at the current work. Each iteration is better and more impactful than the ones before it. The same holds true in building a plan for the courses you play. It takes multiple attempts, wise counsel, and an open mind to arrive at a particular plan. Many touring professionals and their caddies use the same yardage book from year to year and add or change information in their practice rounds. The revision process is an important one, so don't neglect it!

There are several additional items that I want you to consider. Each of these will help provide further insight and helpful tools to aid in modifying your drafts for courses you will play. Revising is more art than science so have some fun with it, and try a few or all of the following items to see what helps you the most.

Item #1: Carry Distance and Rollout. Whenever I do our course management class, I find that most people know their *total* distance on their *best* shot. Great players know their *carry* distance on their *average* shot and sometimes even their *best* shot for both their full, stock, and knockdown shots. Essentially, they really *know* themselves. In addition to this, players often struggle knowing how much rollout (forward or back) they are likely to have. I could write a whole chapter on how your trajectory, carry distance, and the course conditions will influence the ball's final resting place. With that said, let me give you a few guiding principles that will help lead you to considering the best option:

- o Landing the ball on an uphill slope decreases forward rollout, while landing on a downhill slope increases forward rollout.
- o Uphill shots tend to rollout more due to the flatter landing angle, while downhill shots tend to stop faster due to the steeper landing angle.
- o Dry conditions and firmer greens will tend to increase rollout.
- o A curving shot that lands on a slope that is tilted in the same direction will increase the amount of rollout off the slope. For example, a left to right ball flight on left to right sloping ground will increase the rollout down the slope.
- o How much forward or back or right or left rollout you get depends on the specifics of your game. Know precisely how far you are able to carry your ball so you can plan accordingly when deciding where you

want to hit your shots. No two golfers are the same, so don't assume that just because another player's ball stopped quickly that yours will too. Know yourself, and be honest about what you are realistically capable of doing.

Item #2: Change Your Perspective. As a photography enthusiast, it's always intriguing to me to look at my subjects from a different point of view. Finding a new angle, a new lens, or new effects can really help me express and convey to the viewer what it is that I want them to experience and see in the subject matter. Changing the way you look at a golf course or golf hole is a great way to find features that can have a significant effect on your strategy, your confidence, and your score.

I want you to start by looking at a hole backwards. Yes, *backwards*. The green complex has an effect on somewhere near 80% of the shots (approximately 40% of shots are from putting, another 20-30% from inside 100 yards, and 15-20% from approach shots). Given that the most important aspect of a given shot is where your ball ends up, why would we start anywhere else? I encourage the college teams and players I work with to ride the golf course backwards before they even play their practice round. This allows them to see important features and become familiar with the course in a way that they would otherwise not experience in the normal course of play. When possible, this should be your *first* look when building your plan. By starting here, or even just getting the opportunity to look at it this way, you are able to do certain things.

Bradley Klein, PhD., former PGA Tour caddie, shared in *Think Like a Caddy, Play Like a Pro*, "I would walk the course backwards when mapping, always a good way to see the angles and understand the architect's preferred route to the hole."

First, you begin to see things you would normally gloss over like how the contours of the green can help move your ball toward the hole, best place from which to chip and putt, best angle from which to approach different pins, and more.

Second, you begin to build confidence as you become more aware of these items. *Familiarity breeds confidence*. Think of starting a new job, a new school, or traveling to a new place. We exhibit emotions of anxiety, discomfort, and timidity because, though exciting, these things are unfamiliar to us.

While viewing a course backwards heightens your awareness and familiarity with it, not getting any look at the facility can be costly. Everything is unfamiliar from the moment you drive in until the moment you leave. I have heard countless parents of our junior golfers say they just don't travel well, and they have a hard time playing a new course. My first question is always, "Did they get a practice round?" In many cases, they hadn't. That's like saying you were really uncomfortable on a blind date. Of course, you were! You didn't know what to expect. Advances in modern technology can give you an overview of the course, even flyovers, but nothing can replace the experience of being there. The overview is better than nothing, but that's akin to an online-dating profile; you get some information, but not much. You're still going to struggle getting comfortable or making conversation.

Third, looking at the course backwards allows you to see the architect's true purpose of a hole. The ball will eventually come to rest in the hole and nearly every feature of a hole is designed with that end in mind. It's like getting the playbook of the opposing football team's offense and being on their headset the whole game. You can know with great clarity the purpose and design of a hole as it relates to your game. So get a practice round whenever possible, and ask the golf course staff if you can ride the course backwards. Just be courteous when you do and try not to interrupt the normal course of play.

Item #3: Find the Mayor's Office. "The mayor's office" is a term tossed around on the big tours to describe the *flattest* part of the fairway from which to play. This may seem insignificant at first but if you give it some thought, you'll begin to understand why your ball finding this piece of ground on most holes can have a dramatic effect on your score.

Most golfers spend a high percentage of their time practicing from level ground when it comes to the majority of shots outside of 50 yards. This creates a significant gap in experience in playing from level ground to playing from sloped ground. Different lies affect the ball flight depending on your experience and education about these situations. (More on how the lie affects the ball specifically in Course Five.) Experience is a fine teacher but we need more ways to develop our skills from these lies. I'm encouraged to see this being addressed in the instruction world especially with exciting technologies such as ToughLies360.

With that said, and even for those players with degrees of skill like touring professionals, it's almost always preferable to play from a flat lie. There is a certain amount of guesswork involved when playing from uneven lies, and the unpredictability adds another element to try to account for and predict. At times the lie can serve to help a player shape their shots so as to avoid trouble, but in most cases, they provide additional uncertainty about the specific outcome. It's already a game of chance, no need for additional amplifiers to the dispersion pattern. This is also what makes the game exciting, the ability to adjust (which we will spend two courses discussing). Strictly from a scoring standpoint, however, it would behoove all of us to spend as much time as possible enjoying the pleasantness of the mayor's office!

Item #4: Backup Plans. In order to improve your average overall score, it's important that you develop the ability to create backup plans. After all, you will encounter a situation not covered in your original plan, and you should come prepared to adjust to it. You can go overboard when conjuring up alternative strategies, but massaging this aspect of your plan can really save stress and avoid costly little errors that seem to pop up out of nowhere. Keep in mind that businesses, the military, and other successful people and organizations prepare for the "rainy day" or unforeseen circumstances. Being proactive instead of reactive has huge benefits and not just monetarily.

A good backup plan has three key elements: You know your tendencies, you understand likely course scenarios, and you can be creative. You must know your strengths and your weaknesses and how those are amplified on good, average, and bad days. For instance, I have recently become a good driver but I know that if I'm having an off day, that will be the first club to show it. Knowing when I should switch to a different driving club or shot shape on certain tee boxes is crucial. Different course scenarios can also affect my decision to hit driver, fairway wood, or iron. If I have a strong tailwind on my home course on the first hole, I may opt to hit a shorter club than driver, which will get me to the mayor's office as well as keep me in the widest part of the fairway. The prevailing winds on this course would make this a highly likely scenario. Creativity is probably the finest element as it requires you to think outside the box of a good day to the what-if realm of great and bad days. At the time I took my PAT in 2010, I was not a good or confident driver of the golf ball, and I hadn't played a competitive event for nearly two years. I had selected 3 wood/5 iron on many tees should I feel the need to club down. I hit 5 iron more than the driver and 3 wood combined. Knowing the number I needed to shoot and how the course would likely be set up was what led to this particular strategy.[1]

Staying with the driving example, there can be days that are crazy good when you feel completely in control. On these days, you may consider hitting driver on some short par 4s or take a tighter line on a par 5 dogleg to get home in two. These strategies should match up with your personality, so exercise caution here. Also, think of a likely miss or lay-up option on a long par 4 that could give you a good up and down look should something happen outside your normal or desired course of play. Think outside the box when developing your backup plan, as your options are only limited by your imagination. You can't be prepared for every possible scenario, but you can be ready for likely ones.

Case Study: Caddying for Collegiate Golfers

I've had the privilege of caddying for a number of elite players in various qualifiers and tournaments including events

1 I passed my PAT on the first attempt!

such as the U.S. Women's Open qualifier and the U.S. Open Sectional qualifier. My first task is to get a feel for how they've been hitting the ball in the days leading up to the event. I want to know what shots they like the look of, what types of putts they like the most, how confident they feel about their short game, and the different clubs in their bag. I use the range before and after the practice round(s) as well as the rounds themselves to confirm what my player is capable of comfortably doing.

The second objective is to get important details about the golf course. I gather a ton of information about carry distances, lengths from front and back of tee boxes to certain features of the course, preferred angles to certain pins, details about features of the greens, etc. I try to get as much of this information ahead of time where possible. The nicer the facility, the better the yardage books, so I'll often transfer my previously gathered info to that book. For big qualifiers, the pins are marked on the practice round, but I make a plan for alternative pin placements in case the tournament committee or superintendent has a need to move a pin for some reason (inclement weather or green damage the day before the event).

The third objective is to use the practice round to build a plan for the event. First and foremost is picking the best place to aim off the tee to find the mayor's office (when possible). If they can't get the ball in play, nothing else really matters as they are now fighting to avoid bogey or worse. Second is to figure out the best angle from which to approach a particular pin, and where specifically to aim it to give them the best possible opportunity for birdie and to avoid over par holes. It's important that the player trusts me to provide important feedback about what they believe is best for them in order to match it up with what is factually the best thing to do.

My final step is to review the plan. This is the most overlooked feature in creating a plan. Taking the time to review our decisions lets us make sure we didn't miss any important information and that our strategies match. If you're really smart, you'll even take a few minutes after every tournament round to input your stats and review your plan again. Make any necessary adjustments to improve your score from the first day. Take the time to do these things even if you are not a tournament player to get the most out of your game!

I can promise you this: While you may not have a specific plan for your game when it's not a *normal* day, the architect certainly has a plan for you. If you are not prepared for when those times come (good, bad, or indifferent), the defensive design of the golf course will win the battle against your offensive attacks. I love architects and marvel at the genius of their designs but, personally, I'm tired of them having the upper hand. It's high time golfers got on equal footing with them; not just the best of the best, but all of us!

For Advanced Players

Keep your yardage books from every tournament you play. Stack them on a bookshelf or in a filing cabinet where you can pull them out when you need them. You'll want to make edits to them every time you return to these facilities. You will also save yourself the headache of rewriting several of the key features. If you already do this, keep in mind that golf courses do change over time so make sure you confirm the information you've recorded.

One of the mistakes I watch high level players make in refining their plan is that they create their strategies almost exclusively based on how well they hit the ball during the practice round or how they've been hitting it the previous week(s). I mentioned before that I get this information from my players when I'm caddying, but I don't use it as the sole barometer. Your job is to figure out the best way to play the golf course *that day*. Don't assume that because you hit it like a champ or like garbage means that you should play accordingly. I'm looking for the best way for you to play *all of your rounds* that week, not just one. What you did yesterday has no bearing on what you should do tomorrow. Remember that it is a game of chance with likely outcomes.

The last thing I would suggest advanced players do is watch and figure out what the best players around you are doing to play the hole. I cautiously suggest this because I mentioned earlier you have to play with *your* skill set, not theirs. You can, however, learn from the places they tend to put the ball on both their good and bad shots and ask them how they see certain holes. Find out what other great players are doing and figure out which things that they do will be helpful to you. You don't have all the answers, so be coachable!

A suggestion for parents and college coaches: Don't tell your players how to play certain holes, have a discussion with them. *It's not about you being right, it's about what's right for them*. They need to develop their own instincts and learn. Even if you think they are flat out wrong, it's better to strike up a conversation. What you see on the outside doesn't always match what's on the inside. In an interview in 2019 with *Golf*

Channel Morning Drive after winning his 7th national title in 20 years, Duke Head Women's coach Dan Brooks was asked what separates his program from others. He responded, "Help them to be just as independent as possible. Most of the time they are going to be out there by themselves. So we try to help them be very self-sufficient." It's no accident that they continue to be the best program in the country year in and year out.

As coaches and parents, we can learn from our players too. They come at the game with a completely different set of experiences and skills from everyone else. We all have a unique perspective on things and we can learn from each other. After all, we won't live long enough to make all the mistakes ourselves, so we must learn from one another!

The Champions Takeaways

- Review your strategy, don't assume your first draft is your best one.
- Find the mayor's office with your tee shots.
- Look at the golf course backwards to see how the architect has designed the hole to be played.
- Be prepared, consider things that could happen which might affect your strategy.

For Advanced Players

- Hold onto your yardage books, you may need them in the future.
- Make your strategy to make *all your rounds* better, don't make it based solely on how you played in your practice round.

- Learn from other *great* players and coaches; learn from your players, too!

Exercise #4: The Drafting Process

Part 1: Review the plan you created in Assignment #3. Make adjustments to your plan based on the new information presented in this section. In particular, try to get a look at your course in reverse by standing on the green looking back.

Part 2: Create several backup plans for your home course. They could be general for the whole day/round or for a specific hole or shot. Make these notes in your yardage book where appropriate.

When you're thinking like a caddie, there are no automatic decisions in club selection, no reference to what you hit here last time, or what club your opponent is using. Each shot is considered by itself and is informed by the conditions that exist at that particular moment in time.

—James Y. Bartlett, *Think Like a Caddie, Play Like a Pro*

COURSE FIVE: Game Time Decision Making

In sports, as in life, adjustments have to be made. When you go to college, get married, have kids, or move to a new city, state, or country, you must adjust to the new dynamics if you want to be happy and successful. In sports, you're presented with a new defense, a turnover happens, you make an error that puts you significantly behind, or a player gets on a hot streak. In all these circumstances, adjusting to these dynamics is what separates good athletes and coaches from great ones.

All athletics boils down to these two dynamics: being aware and adjusting. I call it "Triple A Athletics." The best *a*thletes are first *a*ware and then they *a*djust. We begin the process of learning to adjust by developing a process by which we can analyze every shot that we face (creating awareness). Before we do this, however, I want to take a moment to review the principles we've covered so far by utilizing a chart I call "The Champions Diagram."

The Champions Diagram summarizes the foundational principles that make up the game of golf. You'll notice that the

Champions Diagram

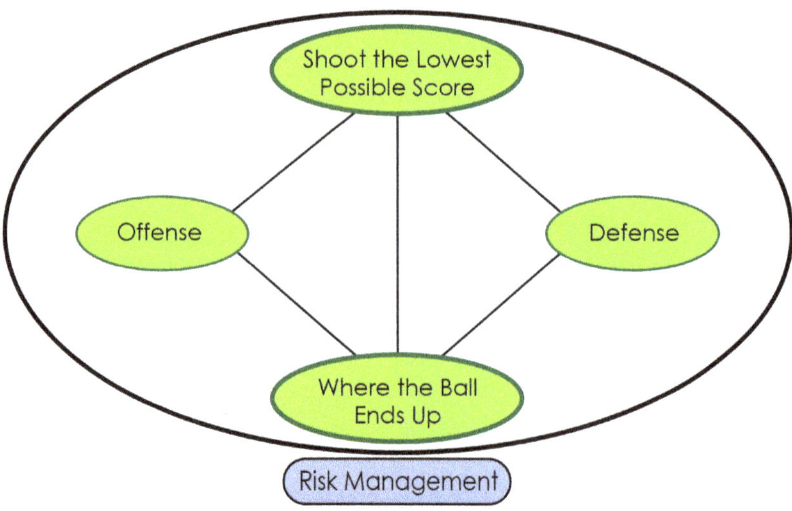

universal objective of shooting the lowest possible score is at the top as it guides every decision you make. Then you have the offense and defense. These two work together to cause this score to happen. They are also the influencers as to where the ball ends up, which is ultimately what causes the score. The oval underneath this whole diagram is to get you to make the lowest possible score happen over *all the rounds* that you play. This is essentially done through risk management, where there is no one right or wrong answer, but simply managing your skill set against the course you are playing. I'll discuss risk management in more detail in the next course. All of these pieces constantly work together to cause your score to happen. If you want to score lower, you must understand how they interact with each other so that you can have some control over what happens.

Case Study: Brett

Brett has been a student of mine since he started college golf. He's had some highs and lows. I'll share more on him on the section on the mental game. I recall a specific moment in 2018 when Brett had just finished a qualifying round. He came up to me and said, "I *don't know what happened*, I got so *unlucky* on 14-16, I *should've* shot even par or better!" First off, when I hear those words in italics uttered, I know that the player is not thinking rationally and likely won't be receptive to me telling them what they should've done. I simply asked him to walk me through what happened. I'll give you a few snippets of this conversation: Brett had 150 in on 14, but he shot the tree in the distance by accident at 184. Ball carries over the green to a nasty place to play from, makes double. Hole 15 is a par 5, he went for it in two. Ball gets buried under the lip of the bunker and he proceeds to take two shots to get out, then doesn't get that up and down, makes bogey. Hole 16 is a long par 3 (220+) with the pin on the back right corner. It's a very difficult green to hit. Brett hits it dead on the flag but it carries to the back of the green and rolls over down about 30 yards from the flag. Makes bogey.

Keep in mind Brett's words: *I don't know. . .unlucky. . . should've.* I walked him through a few things: If he was using a yardage book, he never would've gotten the yardage wrong (at least not that much) on 14. *Should've* made par or better. The Par 5 15th, was that bunker location unlucky? I argue not. I asked Brett how he had hit his wedges earlier in the round and he said, "Really good, almost holed two of them." Brett is not a long hitter and to get the ball on the green in two is unlikely, but the ball could roll into and up under the lip of the bunker. He was also trying to make up for the double on the previous hole. He *should've* made no worse than par and *should've* had a decent look at birdie. On 16 he "felt" he needed to get it to the flag. Blinded by the need to make up for the three or four lost strokes on 14 and 15, he failed to miss that he had nearly 40 yards of green to work with short of the hole. He could've clubbed down and given himself a 30'-40' putt for birdie and have a great chance at par—anything short and left of that flag, he is likely to make par over 80% of the time. He *should've* made par. Instead of Brett being only one or two shots back of the leader, he was now middle of the pack and six shots back.

We've all been in Brett's shoes. We know how out of control we *feel* in these moments. What we are suffering from is not bad ball striking or a weak mental game. It's poor course management. This is where things get dicey. You can make the best plan in the world and still not execute. Once you are finished creating your plan, you are entering the world of "on-the-fly" decision making. Most people, like Brett, have a poor or incomplete process as they face these individual scenarios. The worst part is, if you don't have a base plan to adjust from, then your decisions suffer at the hand of the architect's tactics.

This is where game management gets fun *and* very challenging. There are virtually an infinite number of situations that you'll face in the course of your golfing career, so how can you possibly develop a way to respond to all of them? I have developed a concrete *way of thinking* that will allow you to problem solve in any scenario. Before we take a look at it, I want to share a little experience from my mathematics degree.

In an upper level mathematics course I took in college, called discrete mathematics, we spent a substantial amount of time developing tools to solve certain problems and then prove that they will work *for all* problems for *every* scenario. This is an arduous task to first develop a solution, then prove it for an infinite number of situations. I have developed a 4-step Pre-Shot Checklist that will allow you to answer any and every situation you'll face. It's taken me a number of years to arrive at this, but I know these four questions can lead you to your best solution and allow you to improve your decision-making skills:

Question #1: What is the lie? I believe firmly that the lie is the boss. It can affect distance, change the curve on the ball, change the trajectory, and add or reduce spin. In essence, it tells you what's possible. Too many golfers don't listen to the lie and try to execute a shot that it simply won't allow—try to fade the ball off a draw lie or draw the ball off a fade lie, try to hit a long iron from a lie where the ball sits down in thick rough, try to hit a high flop shot from a very tight lie on a downhill slope. These are just a few examples of poor decision making (unless you have an extremely high degree of skill and the particular situation allows for it).

Both downhill and sidehill lies with the ball below your feet will make the ball curve and/or start to the right. Conversely, both an uphill and a sidehill lie with the ball above your feet will make the ball curve and/or start to the left (opposite is true for lefties). Lies out of the rough generally also reduce the amount of spin on the ball thus decreasing the amount of curvature.

They can influence the clubface significantly at times causing the ball to start more to the right or left. A flyer lie can make the ball launch higher, and thick buried lies out of the rough can make the ball launch lower. There are countless other scenarios regarding the lie. The specifics of these can be learned through practice or by consulting other more experienced players. Before you pull the club out of your bag and swing away, make sure you evaluate what the lie is.

How does the lie affect distance? Here are some basic principles: Let's start with the rough. The ball can sit down or up or somewhere in between. In most cases, the rough will decrease the amount of spin on the ball regardless of the lie. On the cleaner lies, this can cause the ball to appear to "jump off the face," often referred to as a flyer lie. Because of the decreased spin, the ball will tend to carry further and run more. For most other lies out of the rough, the thicker the grass and further the ball sits down, the lower and shorter it will fly and the more rollout it will have. Again, experience is a great teacher here as you acquire the ability to make an educated guess as to what will happen.

You must also consider uphill and downhill lies. Here we can be a little more factual. If you have a lie that is uphill a few degrees, it's like adding a few degrees to the loft of your club. This can turn a would-be 8 iron into a 9 iron, so you may need to club up. The opposite of this is true as a downhill lie of a few degrees could turn your 8 iron into a 7 iron and so you may need to club down.

Question #2: How far is it *really*?! This seems like an elementary question, but it's here that most major problems occur and it's the one that everyone can do. I love rangefinders, but I believe they've crippled many players from figuring the true distance and paying attention to other distance information. We're producing "point and shoot" golfers and skipping critical analytical tools that give us a true distance. In a class at Miles College, we ended up adding more than 20 yards to a shot on a day with 11 mph winds. Most of the guys thought I was crazy for adding that much distance. But as we flesh these pieces out, you'll begin to see that playing point and shoot golf is no good for your game.

There are a list of factors that affect the true distance of a shot: elevation, wind, temperature, and the lie. These items are barely given a thought in the "point and shoot" style of golf that we see today. Thanks to modern technology, we can be more precise about these effects.

For every headwind shot, the wind will affect the ball by 1% of the distance times the miles per hour. This means that on a 150-yard shot with an 8-mph wind in your face, the shot will play 150x.01x8=12 yards further! Not all shots are created equal and tail winds are a little trickier to figure, but this serves as a great starting point. Downwind also straightens out curving ball flights, and headwinds amplify curving ball flights so the effect of a head or tail wind could amplify the distance even further. Experience is a fantastic teacher here. Practice on windy days with a launch monitor to see how much the wind may affect your ball.

Elevation can be a tricky one. With modern range finders able to provide the slope, you can get pretty close to the correct amount of yardage to add or subtract. I want to caution giving

Elevations

Same Elevation

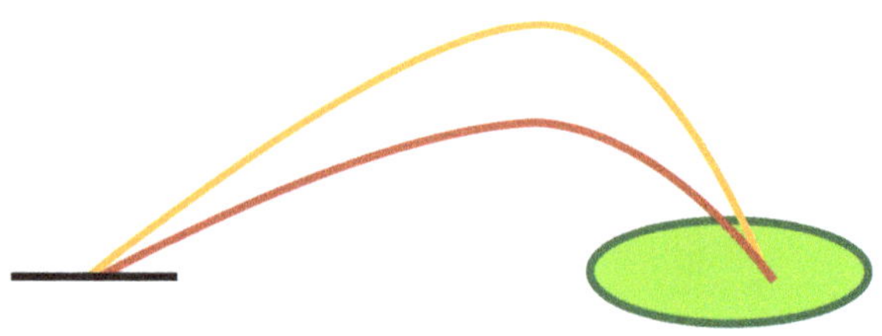

Downhill Elevation Change

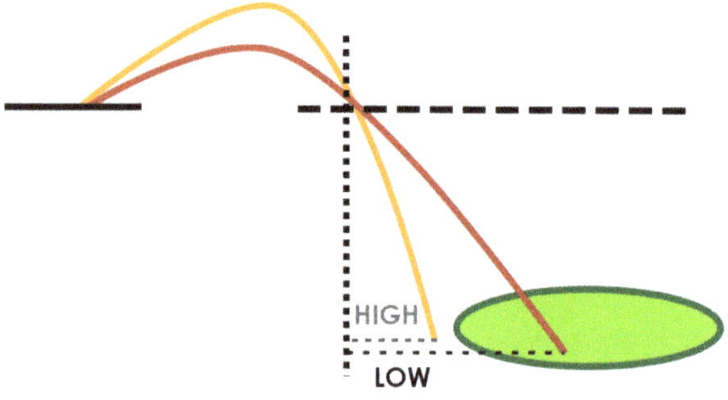

Uphill Elevation Change

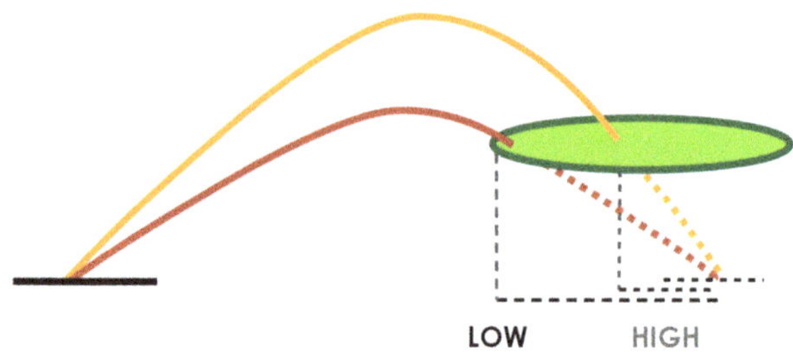

an exact formula here, however, as experience and utilizing your practice rounds are often the best teachers on this subject. When you get into more severe elevation changes, keep in mind that your trajectory will have an effect on the carry *and* total distance. The higher your trajectory, the less effect the elevation has on your ball and vice versa, as you can see from the diagrams.

Downhill elevation changes tend to cause shots to stop faster than uphill ones because the ball is landing at a steeper angle. The opposite is true with uphill shots. Learn specifically how your ball flight is affected by elevation changes, don't just go off what your teammates or opponents do.

Temperature can be a major fooler, especially as we get into the temperatures within 10-20 degrees (Fahrenheit) of freezing. Trackman has shown that 10 degrees of temperature change affects the shot by one yard, assuming all else is equal. When you get into colder temperatures, like below 60, you'll need to keep in mind that the colder it gets the more layers you're wearing which restricts your range of motion. In addition, your muscles will be "colder" which keeps them from stretching fully and making them move more slowly. In severe cold temperatures, you could experience as much as a 20-30 yard loss of distance.

Question #3: Where do I want it? This may seem like an obvious answer: as close to the hole as possible! As discussed earlier, the only thing that matters in shooting the lowest score is where the ball ends up. Remember the exercise in Course Three: Constructing Your Plan, I had you mark where you would want the ball to end up on your tee shots and approach shots to all pin placements? You can utilize this at this juncture to add or subtract distance and move your aim left or right. The circumstances may have changed slightly so you may need to consider adjusting off of your original plan. A helpful way to think through this is by asking yourself two additional questions until you learn to reason properly:

What is preferable? What would you really like to do? High soft fade to a tucked back right pin with a 9 iron? Knock-down straight ball 20 feet left of the flag? Driver down the left middle to give an opportunity to go for it in two? Full 8 iron to the front pin over water? Punch it through the trees with a low hook to run it up on the front of the green? If you could have it your way, what would you do?

There are no limits to this question. Don't think about what the best option or the smartest option is, decide where you want it if you could make that happen. I'd love to have my drive finish on the green on that short par 4 on my home course, or hit a driver long down the fairway so I could have a wedge in on a medium length par 4. I'd like the ball to hug the corner of the dogleg just skirting by to give myself a shorter second shot in on a difficult dogleg left par 4. In some cases, I might just want to be on the green or near the green on a long Par 3 or simply find the fairway off the tee on a narrow but short par 5. The only limit is your imagination. In a lot of circumstances, though, we don't ask this question, or it's the only question we ask so our actions follow with simply "at the pin" or "in the fairway with the longest club possible." The next question leads us to a better answer.

What is practical? When you ask this question, you begin to examine basic probabilities. Is that option the *best* option? Is it the *wise* option? *I don't teach right and wrong to my students in decision making. I teach risk and reward.* The game of golf is simply risk management, and by asking what is practical you begin to think about the true implications of a decision. You'll notice from some of the above examples that the preferable action varies from high risk to low risk. Sometimes the practical lines up with the preferable, but in many cases, it serves as a sort of check on our ego. When we say that a person isn't practical, what we are saying is that their set of expectations don't line up with reality. These people simply choose to ignore reality and tend to experience a great deal of frustration. Keep in mind that disappointment is the gap between expectations and reality. Reality is always there. We must recognize it in order to be genuinely happy and successful. By asking what is practical we begin to examine our own abilities and repertoire of shots.

Altitude also has an effect on how far the ball travels. I remember getting to play at a high elevation in Colorado and was amazed at how much further I hit the ball. Conversely, playing in coastal areas, the ball will travel considerably shorter. If you have access to a launch monitor like Trackman, then use it! The amount varies from player to player and club to club so getting a precise measurement is a must. If you don't have access to this, simply factor in an approximately 5% increase in distance for high elevations.

Question #4: What can I do? This question leads us to decision time. We look at our set of skills, and decide on a course of action we wish to take. I want you to keep in mind one really big thing: *You always have more than one option.* I have yet to find a scenario in which a player doesn't have multiple options. It may not be an option you prefer, but you'll have more than one. Even for the higher handicappers reading this book, you have multiple options in many cases. So how do I know what I can do? How can I see multiple options? It's a mix of three factors: your skill set, your personality, and the difficulty of the shot.

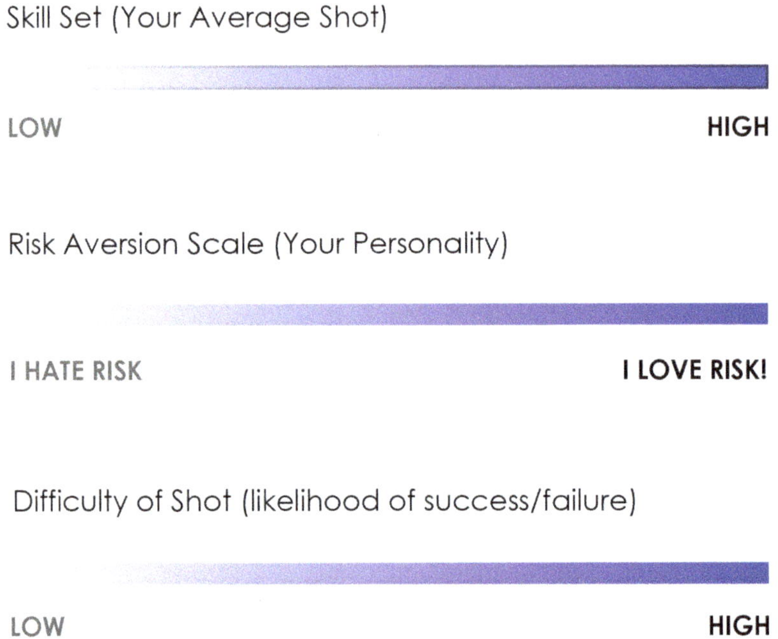

For the first two lines above, put an X on the bar nearest to how you would describe yourself. The information you've gathered in the first several sections of this book, and the stats you've been collecting over the last few weeks will help illuminate the first one. For your skill set, I have my players mark the various aspects of their game along that line with different letters (P for putting, D for driving, I for irons, and so on). The second one is a general read on your personality through the measurement of risk aversion, a term used a great deal in the financial sector. It is simply a measure of how conservative or aggressive your personality tends to be. You may be more aggressive or conservative in different areas of your life but, on the whole, how would you rate yourself? The last scale is on an as-needed basis. Each shot carries with it a certain amount of risk, or probability of success or failure, based on the first two scales.

If you're someone who has a high degree of skill but you are risk averse (conservative) and the difficulty of the shot is high, then you should probably be considering a different shot or target. Why? While your skill set is high even with this difficult shot, your personality is the governing body in this scenario. You may not like the fact that you have to back down from this shot, but trying to hit a shot that is opposite your personality in this situation sets you up for excessive tension, nerves, and doubt, thus leading you to not executing a shot properly. *I believe sound mental training must* ***follow*** *sound decision making*. If you are making decisions that don't line up with your skill set, your personality, or the likely outcome of the shot (understanding those basic principles of probability theory), then you can have all the mental training in the world and still not get any better or be any more confident.

On the other end of the spectrum are people with low skill sets and varying degrees of risk aversion who take on high risk, low success shots regularly. It's absolutely ridiculous when these people (especially those who have aggressive personalities) take on a high percentage of difficult shots and expect to play well! It's just as ridiculous as an elite player expecting to play well tournament after tournament with very aggressive decision making.

What's worse in these scenarios is that on the rare occasion that you do pull off the shot, it drastically over-inflates your perception as to how good you are and you get worse and worse over time and become more and more miserable. In the most extreme cases, you'll leave the game entirely. I have no problem with people taking on or avoiding risk if they understand the decision they are making. If they can explain it to me and can take the outcome on the chin (if it's bad) or with humility (if it's good), then I am completely ok with it because they understand the nature of the game and have, therefore, accepted whatever happens.

This is certainly a lot to consider and may be one of the reasons for the point and shoot style of golf. But let me show you how this played out in an experience I had with the Miles College Golf Team.

CASE STUDY: MILES COLLEGE

This team was a fun group to work with. I started at the green and had two volunteers. Based on their average shot pattern, they decided they needed to add 6 yards to their shot to the front right pin on the 9th green. So we went back in the fairway and selected a shot that was 167 yards. We had an 11-mph wind in our face and slightly from the right, and an elevation change of approximately 2 yards uphill. So here's the math that we performed:

Rangefinder distance: 167 yards

167-4=163 - Accounting for downhill lie

163+2=165 - Accounting for elevation

165+18=183 - Accounting for 11 mph headwind

183+6=189 - Accounting for where the player wants it (understanding average shot)

"True" distance: 189 yards

One of the players went from an 8 iron to hitting a knock-down 5 iron! They both originally thought I was crazy, but were floored when they saw how good their shot patterns were on the green after I had them hit 10 shots each. They mentioned they probably would have clubbed up one club or at most a club and a half. Especially for those playing competitive golf, precision in your distance selection is crucial. Don't be afraid to trust the *real* number.

Once you have figured out what the lie is, where you want it, and what you can do, we have one final step: what you *will* do. I describe this in three parts: commit, rehearse, trust.

Commit. Once you've asked those four questions, you have to decide what you are actually going to do. Upon deciding, *you must commit to the shot fully*. No doubts. If you follow these questions, you will not doubt very often because you have already analyzed your options, removing whatever doubt may have existed. You are essentially saying, "I believe this is the best course of action for me at this moment based on the information provided." I have found that players who used to be unable to commit to the shot or stay focused on the shot are able to focus and commit much better when they've gathered all the information required to arrive at a reasonable solution.

They were often missing information that was leading them to have doubts or uncertainty about what might happen. I am convinced that the "point and shoot" golfers experience this uncertainty because their subconscious brain is sending out warning or caution signals. Depending on the research you find, our brains process between 11 million and 50 million bits of information every second; obviously, most are at the subconscious level. That "I'm just not sure" that you feel inside is often the WARNING DANGER AHEAD signal from your subconscious. My students who have committed to this decision-making process eliminate a substantial amount of doubt and worry when they play. It doesn't remove all nerves, but it certainly serves to calm them and let them commit to a shot in the face of those nerves.

So when you commit to the shot, put all your attention and focus on that shot. This becomes the sole focus of your thoughts, no thoughts about where you don't want to go or what could go wrong, only on what you want to do. Committing can be thought of this way: deciding what you WANT to do, not trying to avoid what you DON'T want to do. If I ask you to *not* think about a red corvette, your mind just thought of a red corvette. If you try to not think about the out of bounds on the right, you'll think about the out of bounds. So think about what you want to do and commit to it.

Rehearse. This one is straightforward. Rehearse a swing or two that feels like you'll hit the shot you've decided. We are giving our brains something to react to. This feel tells your brain, "this is what I want." In a game that can be so stationary, this component can be vital to your success. I'm not a fan of a lot of practice swings (less than three in full shots) except in wedge shots from around the green, as you are creating a very unique shot on the spot with a very specific feel. These wedge shots have the largest degree of variability in the distance and the lie, so take a number of swings until you believe you have made the swing that feels like it will hit the shot you desire.

Trust. Trusting is nothing more than believing that this shot is the best course of action and that you can and will execute it. Yes, it is a game of chance and you play golf with your average shot, but at this moment you must *believe that you can hit the precise shot you have chosen.* Trust comes from practice and sound decision making and a belief in oneself that you can do what it is you're trying to do. Many of the students with whom I've worked on this have found it much easier to trust themselves because they know they've picked the best shot for them in that moment or have chosen to take a little risk, and they are ok doing so. There are countless books on the mental game that teach a slew of various tricks and techniques for being able to trust the shot. I will share some of my favorites that have worked for a large number of my students in the final course.[1]

Before we finish out this section, let me make a note about how this applies to putting. You can use the same four questions above, but most of that is done by feel and experience. I love

---

1 The USGA has been pressing hard on pace of play. Given the large amount of information above it may seem difficult or impossible to get that done in a timely manner. A couple of things you should consider. First, make this a habit and you'll be able to breeze through the questions very quickly. Two, this is why planning ahead and making a plan is critical. If you already have a plan for where you want the ball, it'll save you a large amount of time and stress. Lastly, be thinking of these things as you are approaching your ball. You can already have a general idea of how far you might be, how the wind is behaving, what the lie is, and what you may want to do before you arrive at your ball. Once you get there you can flow quickly through all four questions and go!

what Hank Johnson teaches here, as it matches perfectly with the principles above. He has players use the words Speed, Read, Aim, Speed. Before you ever decide the line you want to take, you must first determine how hard you plan to hit it. Do you like to die it in the hole, hit the back of the cup, or somewhere in between? Usually the speed will match a player's personality, but not always. Aggressive personalities tend to be back-of-the-cup style putters, and conservative personalities tend to be die-it-in style putters. Regardless, you must decide your speed before you decide on your read. Every great player is assuming a certain speed when they are picking the line, whether it's conscious or not. It doesn't have to be specific; it may just be a feel that you have. The second thing to do is to read the putt and determine where you will need to aim the ball in order for it to go in based on the speed you have chosen. Third is aim. Aim your ball, the line on your putter, and your body lines square (unless deemed otherwise by your instructor) to your intended target line. Lastly is speed again. This is for when you make the stroke. The only thought you should have when making the stroke is to roll the ball the right speed as the line was taken care of during the aim portion. Poor putters are almost always too line focused during the stroke. If you struggle starting your putts on line, get into a practice regimen that gets you great at starting the ball on line. This will allow you to focus on the speed when making your stroke. This is a fantastic routine and should help you hole more putts more often and make it easier to learn from your mistakes.

So the first step in learning to adjust is to have a process that allows you to analyze the changing dynamics of the game. Remember that great athletes are first aware and then they adjust. You will face new situations almost daily and having a plan to handle them is a must. Practice this process on the range and in your casual rounds of play and soon it will become a habit that you work through in a matter of seconds. You'll find yourself more committed to what you want and find the ball ending up in much more favorable positions more often. You might even find those nerves calming down some when you play!

For Advanced Players

The thing I see most with elite players is assuming they are already good at course management. Raymond Floyd had a rude awakening when he made it onto the big tour. He was strong, confident, and highly skilled. What he quickly realized after struggling his first year on the PGA Tour was how much better the experienced tour players were at course management than he was. Raymond finally let go of his pride and learned how to play some great golf. It wasn't that he didn't have the physical skills. It was that he was poor at course management.

The only thing worse than poor course management is assuming you can be skilled enough where you don't need great strategy. I've never met a player that is so skilled that they can disregard this area of the game. You cannot hit it far enough, close enough, or make so many putts that you don't or won't need this. You might be able to do this once a year at best, but you can't do it over and over again. If you're thinking, "I get away with it all the time," you are assuming that will continue as you play better and better players at harder and harder courses under increasingly difficult tournament setups. At some point it won't continue. You might even make it onto the PGA Tour and win a tournament or two, but you won't be able to stay out there! That's the best thing that can happen to you. If you don't accept that course management is a necessary part of your development, then you'll likely never learn because you will have developed bad decision-making habits that will continue to burn you time and time again.

You *need* to have a pre-shot routine that allows you to gather all the necessary information and then make a decision that will work for you. Remember how I talked about getting in the habit of using a yardage book? For those that rarely use one, when you finally have one, you don't really have a process of sorting through and dealing with all of this information. If you do, it takes way too long for you to process it. These four questions—What is the lie? How far is it? Where do I want it? What can I do?—should be able to be processed very quickly. The only way to do this is to make it a habit! Even if you don't use these specific questions, you need a process that allows you to sort through large amounts of data quickly. I'm with Brooks Koepka on this one: "What's taking you so long?!" Just like Aimpoint Express is meant to be a quick read of the greens, this process should be done quickly.

If you don't have this kind of process in your game, develop this one and commit to doing it every time you play. If your pre-shot routine has some of these elements but not all of them, put the missing element in and commit to using it daily. In the words of Aristotle, "Success is never an accident. It is always the result of high intention, sincere effort, and intelligent execution." Be intelligent and use this process, there will never be a situation where you can't use it!

The Champions Takeaways

- Use this 4-step process to come to the best decision on every shot you hit:
  - What is the lie?
  - How far is it?
  - Where do I want it?
  - What can I do?
- Use a similar thought process in putting:
  - Decide your speed first.
  - Pick your read (line) second.

- o Aim the ball and club third.
- o Focus on and make the stroke for speed.

For Advanced Players

- o Don't assume you are good at course management.
- o Develop a process to analyze all the necessary information quickly and accurately.

Exercise #5: Habituate Your Thought Process

From here on, use the process described in the preceding pages for every shot you hit. Even in putting, decide on things like the speed you want to roll the ball before you just step up and hit it. No more point and shoot golf! Record your experience of the next 18-54 holes in your practice journal or notebook. Do this process until it's as familiar to you as walking.

"I never played a round when I didn't learn something new about the game."

—Ben Hogan

COURSE SIX: Developing Your Instincts

EXPERIENCE IS ONE OF THE GREATEST TEACHERS AS LONG AS IT'S TEMPERED BY HUMBLE REASONING. An ego that is unwilling to see the facts of a matter and accept the good and bad of them will always struggle to improve. This experience combined with self-reflection opens up a world of possibilities that will set you on a path of constant improvement. Hank has always told me, "You can't get 10 years of experience in a day less than 10 years, but you can improve the quality of that experience." As you continue through the final courses of this book and continually apply these principles, you'll find that the quality of your experience is maximized. Course Five's focus was on what you need to do while you play. Learning to develop your instincts is a matter of two additional items: self-reflection and playing with what you have *that day*.

In Course One, I asked you to get connected to a stat tracking program and use it with each round that you play. This will serve as your starting point for self-reflection. Analyzing statistical data can be difficult, especially for those not mathematically minded. I want to give you a systematic way of looking at your stats. Start with the score and work from the green back to the tee, just as you were asked to do in developing your strategy.

Let's say you shot 81. Your stats were as follows: 35 putts, 3/10 up and downs, 8 greens in regulation (with one birdie), 10 fairways in regulation. The first error is that you had 35 putts. If you improve in that area by just a few, you could've shot in the 70s. Second, you failed to get up and down for par 7 out of the 10 times you missed the green. Improving this would directly affect your putting as you would have 1 putt instead of 2 or more on each of those holes. Third, you hit 8 greens in regulation which meant you had 8 opportunities for birdie but you only made 1 of those. Lastly, your stats looked pretty good with 10 fairways in regulation. This first glance at stats will always tell you *what* happened, but not necessarily *why* it happened. Further analysis is needed to get to the bottom of it.

Why did you have 35 putts? Let's assume you didn't have any 3-putts and that you made all of your putts inside of four feet. That tells me that your wedge play from around the green didn't get the ball close to the hole very often. *Why* didn't you get the ball close to the hole? Are you "just bad at chipping" or did you leave yourself in difficult places from which to get up and down? Were you short-sided, buried in a bunker, or did you have any easy chips from across the green? Perhaps it's a combination of the above, but you *need* to know this! In many cases, people leave themselves with difficult pitches especially since a majority of people have poor strategy. This means we need to go a step further: *Why* did you short-side yourself those few times or miss the green? Did you fail to account for your average shot? Miscalculate the wind or elevation? Did you have a difficult lie? Miss key pieces of information? Did a missed fairway make it difficult or impossible for you to hit the green? Or did you just hit a bad shot? You missed 4 fairways in that round, where did that put you? *Why* did you miss the fairway? Could you have selected a different shot, etc.?

I get tired of people finishing rounds and saying "I couldn't buy a putt" or "I didn't hit anything solid" or "If I could just hit a fairway." The reason I get fed up with it is that they will go out and make the same mistakes over and over again because they are so *biased* and *blinded* by their emotions, *even* when they have stats! Start with the facts around the green and work your way back. Search for the *real why* for your performance problems.

One major error that I see players make is that they start with why instead of what. When you start with why, it's most often based in emotions, both good and bad. It's not that your emotions make you incorrect in your analysis of your round, it's just that they often taint what actually happened. We begin to see things not as they are, but as we want them to be. Let's take a look at a case study from a recent experience I had with a player.

Case Study: Grant, "If only. . ."

"My putting is killing me. If I could just putt. . ." This is almost never *the only* problem. This was from one of our talented juniors playing a fairly large regional event. I made sure I got the stats:

- Score 79/Par 72
- 8 bogies, 1 birdie, 9 pars

- o 50% greens in regulation
- o 14% missed right, 14% missed left, 22% missed short. All misses were within 10 yards of the edge of the green except one (20+ yards), half were within 5 yards of the edge of the green.
- o Average proximity to the hole was 40 feet.
- o Closest birdie putt was 11 feet, four birdies were between 11-15 feet.
- o 57% fairways in regulation
- o Five misses left of the fairway, one miss right of the fairway. All misses were within 9 yards of the edge of the fairway with four of those being inside of 6 yards.
- o No penalty strokes
- o Hit two shots in the greenside bunker: 0/2 up and down.
- o All chips and pitches finished outside 3 feet.
- o He had 33 putts and strokes *lost* putting was 4.02 (to the average PGA Tour player).
- o Average leave on putts outside of 15 feet was 4 feet.

Here's what I see from these stats. This young player had a "good round" with no major errors. Missing greens wasn't a major factor due to the small misses, but there was a significant number left short of the green. Pitching the ball closer to the hole would have resulted in a lower score. This player continued to have putts from outside 4 feet to save par which, had this been closer to the hole, par was virtually guaranteed. Putting was a significant factor, but not to the degree that the player had assumed. Losing 4 strokes sounds like a lot, but not when you realize that's relative to the average PGA Tour player. My conclusion from these numbers alone leads me to believe that a lower score could've been achieved most effectively by hitting a few more greens in regulation, pitching the ball closer to the hole, and making a few more putts. Obviously, improvements in every stat category could make an improvement, but I'm looking for the most significant reasons.

These stats are great and they begin to give me a vague idea of why the score was 79, but the picture is still really cloudy. A few questions I have about this round would be: How difficult were the pitches? When a fairway was missed, what kind of angle, lie, or shot was left? What was the mental state of the player? Was there an effective pre-shot routine to analyze each shot? Where was the player trying to hit the ball relative to where it ended up? Was the player aware of the feel of their swing on good and bad shots? These types of questions are what illuminate the why of each round and of a particular shot. The statistics of your rounds give you a concrete place to start, and then you need to subjectively take a look at what led to those numbers.

The next question I get is this: Now that I have these numbers, how do I figure out the *real* why? How do I guarantee that I'm looking through a clear set of lenses? As I mentioned in earlier courses, we all have some biases and we have to be careful. They can certainly be correct as you are developing your own instincts, but you have to be careful that they don't blind you to what is really going on. Many of the PGA and LPGA Tour players talk about their "team," the group of people in their inner circle who have a say in what's going on. This team helps them make sure they are doing everything they can to play at their best. If you have an instructor, coach, or great players in your small group, you can certainly get input from them. If you do not (or even if you do), you'll need a way to look at your rounds as objectively as possible. I ask all of my players to look at their rounds or certain individual shots or holes by asking a few simple questions:

- **What happened?** This is the factual "data" component like what the ball did, where it ended up, how solidly you hit it, etc.
- **Did I have a plan?** This refers to both the plan you make ahead of the round and the individual decisions you make throughout the round.
- **Was I focused/committed?** After you had a plan, were you able to maintain focus on what you wanted the ball to do? I'm talking 100% free and clear, no distractions from the outside or inside your mind.
- **Was the outcome one of my likely shots?** How are you hitting it *that* day? Is the shot one of the likely ones we established in the first course? This goes for good shots, bad shots, and every shot in between.
- **Was there an alternative or better plan?** Remember you *always* have options. Even on some of the good outcomes, there may have been a better plan and you just got lucky. Or you may have had a great plan, but could an alternative one have helped you?

Before I explain these further, let me be clear about one thing: You do not have to do this to *every* shot you hit. As you think over your rounds and review your data, look at some of the good and bad things that happened and work through these questions. Let me show you how this plays out.

Case Study: Stephenie, Something's Missing. . .

Question 1: What Happened? I was doing a course management lesson with one of my elite college players, Stephenie, one day. She was having a slight miss of a push to the right that she's not accustomed to seeing. Now one miss to the right doesn't mean she's having an off day, but five misses right in the first 3.5 holes does represent an off day. During the course of this lesson, we made some minor adjustments to her strategy to account for the miss to the right (5-7 yard push with irons and 10-15 yard push with the driver). Since it was a lesson, we could work through this process during the round to make adjustments and more post round.

We quickly went through the first three questions for all her shots. We know what happened, she had a plan, she was committed to that decision, and remained focused on the shot. Question 4 looks a little different. Was the push one of her likely shots? Yes and no. On her average day when she's swinging well, the answer is no. However, *that day* it was one of her likely misses. Because the miss was small, we can adjust off of the original plan. This leads to Question 5: Was there an alternative plan? For a few shots on holes 1, 3, 4, 12, and 13, there was an alternative plan to the one we made which would have resulted in a better outcome. I say "we" because while I was letting her make most of the decisions to see her reasoning process, I had the option to override her decision. We both got to learn something! She learned how to adjust, and it helped me reinforce the importance of the principles and processes in this book.

Question 2: Did I have a plan? If you don't have a specific plan beyond "point and shoot," then the question asking stops there. If you don't have that nothing else matters. Regardless of a good or bad outcome, having a plan is the first step in playing your best golf. For Stephenie, we established that she didn't have a specific plan to play any of the holes or hole locations *ahead of time*. She had played the course multiple times, but never built a yardage book with which she could make decisions and adjust accordingly. While you don't *need* this when you play a course, it makes working through the pre-shot routine checklist more difficult, especially when you're having an off day. It makes it harder to come to the *best* solution for that day or week.

Question 3: Was I focused/committed? If you get this far but the answer is no, then again, the remaining questions don't matter. You might consider why you weren't focused, and it could be that there was a better solution or information you hadn't considered as you stand over it. Or you were simply focused on something other than what you *want* to do. More on this in the final course.

Questions 4 and 5: Was it likely to happen? Was there an alternative? If it was a likely outcome but you didn't like what it was, then you might want to consider an alternative. There are times, though, when the alternative options are worse. Remember there are no "rules" that say you have to do this or that like hit it on the green, in the fairway, as far as possible, or in the middle of the green. There is only risk and reward. Regardless of whether it was likely or not, there is always an alternative, whether better or worse. Keep in mind, *sometimes you just hit a bad shot*. If you get all the way through these questions and the ball ended up in a bad place, then it's just a bad shot, simple as that. That's part of the game, and it's a part of life.

This is why outside feedback on rounds is tricky. I never presume what a player was doing or trying to do because I don't have all the information. I may try to infer certain things based on the outcome and even offer some alternative considerations, but I can't assume I *know* the right answer. Even if I'm caddying for them, I don't know how focused they are while over the ball because I can't read minds. Only the player has all the information. Parents, peers, teachers, and coaches that start telling players they shouldn't have done x, y, or z are setting themselves and their players up for failure, disappointment, frustration, and a slew of other negative emotions that can hurt players. The best coaches that I've seen or read about teach their players to be independent and able to reason through situations in sport and life. You cannot separate the two. The same problem-solving skills in golf extend to those in life as well.

Remember this: When you look at your stats, you must also do your best to remove any bias that is trying to protect your ego. If you need help with this, just ask a friend/teammate, instructor, or coach as they will be able to look at the data with a fresh set of eyes. Look at what happened and continue to ask *why* until you come to a reasonable solution.

Coaches and instructors: *This applies to you as well!* Talk with your players about *why* the stats were what they were. Do not assume anything. . .and don't *tell* them what to do. Ask *why* and *lead them* (or let them lead you) to the "right" answer or a better solution.

For Advanced Players

Remember that great athletes do two things: They are first aware and then have the ability to adjust. The problem I see with this group is a continual adjusting without proper awareness. If you are aware of something, but it's the wrong thing, then you begin adjusting your swing, thoughts, or strategy in such a way that it begins to damage your performance. In the worst circumstances, it'll derail players for months or years before they can ever get it back. This awareness goes really deep; a whole book could be written on this alone. I'm convinced this is one of the reasons you see elite players make it to the mini tours or Web.com Tour but struggle to go any further.

The five questions presented previously really help eliminate this type of poor judgment. Making adjustments while you are playing is a challenging endeavor in which a lot must be known about the particular situation, your personality and your abilities. One of the best principles I've heard and put into practice with a few students is to have them mark in a small notebook two things: the shot they were trying to hit, and the shot they actually hit. Great players recognize early on what kind of day it is likely to be and they account for it in their strategy. When making note of these two things, you are able to see more clearly what shots you actually have that day. If the shot continually misaligns with what you desire, then you should consider making a slight adjustment in your strategy.

Case Study: Ali and Connor

Ali is an elite level junior golfer and Connor a mini-tour player. Connor came to the course warmed up intending to play a fade, while Ali came to the course warmed up intending to hit a draw. In Connor's warm-up session, he hit a high percentage of straight shots, a few draws, and a few fades. Ali had a lesson that morning and hit a high percentage of fades during the session. In fact, she had been hitting fades two weeks prior as well. (Note: she was in the process of learning to hit the draw, prefers the draw, but it was not yet a habit.)

Both players step foot on the first tee having made the same error—they weren't aware of the shots they were *actually* hitting. Ali aimed for her draw and Connor aimed for his fade. Connor's ball drew into the left rough, Ali's ball faded off to the right side of the fairway. This pattern continued to happen over the next several holes. After talking with Connor on the fifth tee box, I mentioned to him that I wanted him to aim for the draw, which surprised him. We reflected back and saw that all he had hit was draws. Connor had failed to recognize what his pattern was and continued to miss it left, and short-sided himself in many cases.

On my day with Ali, I decided to tell her exactly where to hit each shot. I knew she was trying to hit a draw and didn't stop her from trying, but I did aim her for a fade on every shot. She was frustrated that she continued to hit that 5-10 yard fade.

In both cases, I wanted them to learn to adjust to what they had that day. Connor began adjusting after we recognized the pattern and in Ali's case, I recognized it for her on the range and aimed her for it. It should be noted that during the six holes I "caddied" for Ali, she was 3-under, something she had never done. The most surprising part of all was that she was still frustrated after those six holes, even though she was 3-under par! Equally surprising is that Connor kept trying to fade the ball when he spent 4 straight holes drawing the ball! This is a case of misaligned beliefs about the game for both players. Their actions reflect that in order to play great golf you have to hit your best or desired shots. While this can help, it certainly isn't true of the game in its entirety. Connor has since developed the process of noting his shot pattern in the early parts of the round and on the range so he can be ready to adjust his plan accordingly. Ali has continued to work hard on her game and has gone on to play college golf at a D1 program.

One of the things I try to make sure my players do is to understand *their* tendencies when it comes to technical errors. The better they get at feeling and being aware when these things are off and what they cause the ball to do, the more apt they are to make correct adjustments on the fly. If you become obsessed about your *swing* on the golf course, you will likely never get to the level you want. It's ok to pay attention to what you're feeling as the round progresses and utilize those feels to help you make small adjustments as you play. But once you are over the ball, your mind should be entirely on the shot.

When it comes to adjusting, make sure the adjustments are small and reasonable. Continue to adjust as needed remembering first that sticking to your original plan is going to be a *great* option in many cases. Preparation is important here as well. If you have a defined plan of how you wish to play the course, then you will have something to adjust from. It's hard to make up the entire thing as you go and have regular success doing so. Remember, the only thing that matters is getting the ball in the hole in the fewest number of strokes possible. That must govern *every* decision you make, especially when deciding whether to adjust or not.

The Champions Takeaways

- o Self-reflection and learning to adjust are keys to continual learning.
- o Track your stats in every round you play.
- o Stats tell you *what* happened, but they don't tell you *why* it happened.
- o Use this 5-step process to review certain shots, holes, rounds:
  - o What happened?
  - o Did I have a plan?
  - o Was I focused and committed?
  - o Was the outcome one of my likely shots?
  - o Was there an alternative or better plan?
- o Consider journaling what you learned each time you play.

For Advanced Players

- o Learn to adjust on the fly by being aware of your tendencies and making small adjustments.

Exercise #6: Reviewing Your Rounds

Take a few minutes to review your most recent rounds with the stats you've collected. Utilize the five questions presented above to work through and make notes. I ask all of my top junior and college players to keep some sort of journal on their rounds. It serves to help them sort through and process what they are learning and makes it easier to remember.

If you want to play your best golf, especially if you are an aspiring or active college or tour player, you would be wise to start making notes and reviewing what you are doing to make sure it is in your best interest. Remember, "Success is never an accident."

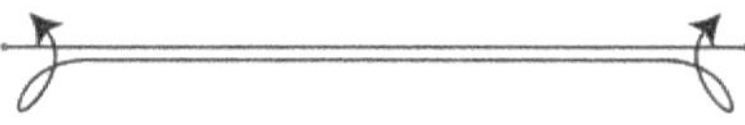

Golf is about how well you accept, respond to, and score with your misses much more than it is a game of your perfect shots.

—Dr. Bob Rotella

COURSE SEVEN: MIND CONTROL

EARLY ON IN THIS BOOK I MENTIONED TWO IMPORTANT THINGS: Beliefs affect behavior, and sound course management must *precede* sound mental training. In this final course, I want to share with you some personal success stories that will benefit you.

A few years ago, someone gifted me a book called *Burn Your Goals*. It was a wonderful book that I highly suggest you read, but the part that stood out to me the most is a section that asked you to fill in the blank of the following phrases:

People are: ______________________

Women are: ______________________

Men are: ______________________

Life is: ______________________

I did it immediately and went with my gut instinct. My answers were embarrassing, to say the least. It went on to say effectively that what you believe is what you attract and how you will act. I was not in a good place mentally or spiritually at the time, having become such a workaholic that I had neglected to take care of my health and my family. My answers to these questions and many more I would reflect upon was what I saw in people and situations. I saw things and acted in accordance with my beliefs at the time. Every time I look back, I am reminded of a time in my life I don't ever want to return to. I have realigned my beliefs and set people around me who will help me make sure that I continue to believe those things and live according to them to the best of my ability.

I have read many of Dr. Bob Rotella's books, and the thing I continue to see in them is an effort to realign your beliefs about yourself and the game of golf. The idea of playing with your misses, covered in the book *Golf is not a Game of Perfect*, matches the statistical truths of probability theory and game theory. When I look at the decisions that people make on the golf course and hear the phrases they use when discussing the game, I get a pretty clear picture about what they believe.

Let's take a moment to review what we've learned so far and see how it leads us to where we are:

We began by talking about how the universal question "What did you shoot?" must govern every decision you make in order to play your best golf. We then discussed how golf is a game of averages with each player and shot they select having a certain percentage chance of hitting the desired shot. Players who understand this make very different decisions than those who don't. They take a deeper look at what they can really do, and what the architect has presented to them, to come to the most optimal decision in that moment. When you hold these beliefs, and you don't execute it at the level you wanted, you are more accepting of the outcome and switch into getting ready for the next shot that awaits you. When you realize that the architect is really smart and has the upper hand, you take a closer look and build a plan to play the golf course, developing a process that allows you to handle every situation you'll face. When you are wrapped up in trying to shoot your very best score and know that you come at every situation with your own biases, you develop a regular process of reviewing your stats and the decisions you make. All of these things lead to happy golfers with lower scores, without a long list of mental exercises to make your frustrated ego more confident.

If you pick a shot that has a high percentage chance of ending up in an undesirable place, and you expect that ball to end up in a good place just because you tried to be more confident, but some part of you deep down is still afraid of hitting a bad shot, then you probably won't pull it off or be able to overcome that fear. The longer I teach golf, the more amazed I am at how much happens at the subconscious level. I've taken players who can't hit a green with perfect swings and switched them into focusing on the shot and staying locked onto it, and the brain responds and makes the ball go there while making the misses smaller. I have also watched these players still struggle to execute on the course because a part of them knows deep down what's not likely to happen. I have guided countless players in changing their strategies and processes, which has led them to being more confident and comfortable on the course. I have heard and read that in various players, the brain processes millions (sometimes tens of millions) of bits of information every second. The evidence is strong in golfers that I've watched and taught that poor decision making is the root cause of a lot of the low confidence and anxiety on the course.

Start by learning to make great decisions and learn from your mistakes. I promise you that if you do these things, you'll be more confident and play better golf.

With all that said, though, the mental game does have a place. People are afraid of poor performance for a variety of reasons, like being concerned with what a parent, peer, coach, or "the world" thinks of them if they perform poorly. The best place I believe you can start is discovering *who* you are and *who* you want to be. These things can't be performance based, they must be character traits, like I am strong, brave, compassionate, hardworking, empathetic, generous, etc.

Hank gives a talk at a charity event each year called the Bradley Johnson Memorial Tournament, which is the top high school invitational event in Alabama. He shares the same message year after year: "Golf is not *who* you are, it's just something that you *do*." If your performance is who you are, then you can just walk around and introduce yourself based on what you shot that week: "Hi, I'm 77, nice to meet you," "Hi, I'm 93, and I'm terrible." I don't think you'll ever play your very best golf if you don't deal with this mental component. Find a psychologist who can help you get to that before you fix the stuff on the surface. Get to know *who* you are and develop great strategy before you start putting band aids on the symptoms of bigger problems. I want to leave you with a few helpful "mental game" tips that I've used to effectively help players execute better.

While I want you to understand that you have an average of shots you're likely to hit and make decisions and take and avoid risks based upon this, I want you to *believe* you are going to hit your best shot! The only way to do this is by focusing on *what you want to do*. The pre-round strategies and on-the-fly decisions you make are already accounting for your average and what you *don't* want to do. They ultimately lead you to what it is that you really *want to do*. You can focus on this a number of ways, but I'll share two:

One is called a "clear key." A clear key is something you think about that doesn't let anything else in. I've watched Hank use this countless times with elite college and tour players; it often revolves around something like the yardage they are trying to hit. They continue to say *the yardage* in their head over and over which keeps their mind "clear" from other thoughts. Another type of clear key is describing the shot over and over in short phrases like "5-yard cut off the pine tree." This clear key is helpful to many players, but it's been especially helpful to my players who struggle to see pictures and visualize shots. Funny side note: One of my college teammates sang to himself under his breath on holes he did not want to go right. He sang the lines from Beyonce's *Irreplaceable*, "To the left, to the left, everything you own in the box to the left." To my recollection, he never hit it right in those scenarios. Athletes find a way to adjust and make something happen. Whatever makes it work!

Second is simple visualization. I have had several players who describe the shot out loud to me in as much detail as they can. The more specific the better as it makes the image more vivid and easier to focus on. I train them to switch on the range from thoughts about the swing to thoughts about the shot. Once they've selected the shot, I ask them to hold that picture in their minds while they are making practice swings all the way up until after they make contact with the ball. If at any point, they lose the picture or it becomes fuzzy, they have to back off. Learning to be disciplined like this in practice makes it a lot easier to take on the golf course.

We all need to become "tougher" and have the ability to "make things happen" when we need to. This is done by putting pressure in your practice. Most golfers make their practice too easy. Put in competitions and challenges against yourself or other players in your practices, and find creative ways to make your practice difficult. If you can complete the activities every time and always win the competitions, then it's too easy. The game of golf is a lot "meaner" than that and you need to be ready for it! Don't go overboard and make it to the point that you won't ever be successful, that'll just leave you frustrated. Your challenges should be just out of reach, but not out of sight. As you are able to complete them, make them harder.

Finally, about confidence. If you struggle to feel confident, start acting confident. Think of confident people you know and the mannerisms they exhibit like the way they walk, talk, stand, sit, etc. They take up a lot of space, speak firmly, walk assertively and where they please, they stand tall, and they tend to smile more. It's been proven time and again that the way you act outwardly can change the way you feel inwardly. Remember Brett from earlier in my book? Brett went from a red-shirt freshman who was in the bottom half of the squad to being voted captain of his college team at the start of his sophomore year, and he qualified for all but one of his events that season! If you look at his swing, it hardly changed. We spent that entire summer working on changing his body language, and it's made a world of difference in his performance. It started by walking around downtown Birmingham one night at the end of his freshman year. We were out to dinner with his family, and when we were headed back to our cars, Brett was walking straight for another guy walking his way. Brett moved aside as the other guy stayed his course. I said "Brett! Why did you move?! We just spent the last 90 minutes talking about body language!" As fate would have it, Brett would have a chance to redeem himself about 30 seconds later as a guy about 50 pounds heavier and about 10 inches taller than him walking with his girlfriend was headed straight for him. I whispered from beside Brett, "Don't move! Stay your course!" To his surprise (really all of ours, as the guy would have knocked him down had they run into each other), the guy moved, even nudging his girlfriend aside, and continued on. As soon as the guy was out of earshot, Brett said "Oh my gosh, that was SO uncomfortable!" What Brett quickly realized was that he could change the way he felt by changing the way he looked, and that it would affect other people around him as well. Don't go overboard with this by intentionally walking into people. The point is simply to change the way you look on the outside to change the way you feel on the inside!

If after all of this you are still unhappy with your performance, find a qualified instructor who has *a history* of making players *better*. They or their students should be able to back that up with hard data. If this course management content didn't work in person, in the classes and lessons I tested it in, then I wouldn't be writing this book. It is based on hard evidence of people improving their scores by more than 3.25 strokes in just a few weeks of applying the principles. I can take you even further if I can see you in person, as I can specifically adapt the content to your game and personality. Remember, too, that you need to discover *who* you are before you get into tips and tricks on how to be more confident. Confidence comes by doing and believing that you can and will do it again!

I wish all of you the very best in playing better golf! Change your beliefs, change your habits, and you'll change your scores for the better. I won't guarantee every round will be lower but I know your average will come down and your happiness and tournament wins will go up. If you want more than this, I would love to help you. I want the best version of you to come out every time you play. Golf is truly a game for a lifetime, and one in which you will never stop learning new things. I look forward to hearing from you and helping you play the golf of your dreams!

FOR ADVANCED PLAYERS

Let's talk mental toughness as it relates to great strategy. If you are in the category who can't help but keep track of where you are in relation to par or the field, then this is for you. If you are one who makes birdies early or late or can't put two nines together, this is for you, too. The thing you need to do is change the game.

My favorite drill (now no longer top-secret) is to go and play what I call the "Birdie Game." My very best players with the highest birdie numbers and thus lowest scores have attempted and completed this game, as it gets them focused on making birdies.

Birdie Game

This is a completion drill. The goal is to finish all 18 holes. The first level is to make a birdie every four holes. Break your scorecard into 4 hole segments (you'll have two holes left over: 17/18). In order to "unlock" holes 5-8, you have to make a birdie somewhere on holes 1-4. In order to advance to holes 9-12, you have to make a birdie on holes 5-8 and so on until you're able to finish. If you fail at any point, you *must* start over at hole #1. *There are no carryovers!* If you make 2 birdies on holes 1-4, you do not get a by or pass on 5-8. I don't care how good you are playing or if you'll have enough time to try again that day or if the course has enough time slots on the tee for you to try again. The only way you'll be able to complete this game is to have great strategy (not too aggressive or conservative), and find a way to dig down and make something happen, like chipping in on your 8th hole to unlock holes 9-12. If you say "I'll just play my way into the clubhouse," you won't get the benefit. This "walk of shame" is hard to deal with and you might even get people asking you questions, but it's a necessary part of this exercise.

Once you can complete this (finish all 18) two or three different times, then try it at 3 holes. Birdie on 1-3 unlocks 4-6. Birdie on 4-6 unlocks 7-9 and so on.

The players I've had do this game stop worrying about making bogies and doubles and start making many more birdies. If you're trying to make the big tours (LPGA, PGA), then you better be doing this drill. You'll stop being afraid of making mistakes because they don't hurt you in the Birdie Game.

With the players I have do this, I am always and only

concerned about them getting their birdie count as high as possible. The first question I ask them after every tournament round is "How many birdies did you make?" The final score matters to me, but I want all their mental energy on making birdies and the best way to do it. You'll also learn how and when to take aggressive lines, and when you'll have to rely on a chip in or making a long putt to make birdie. You'll develop grit, focus, have more fun and make *way* more birdies on your way to lower scores and bigger trophies. Now go out there and get it done. You can do it!

The Champions Takeaways

- Beliefs affect your behavior.
- Good strategy precedes and coincides with the mental game.
- Use a clear key or visualization to stay focused on what you *want to do.*
- If you want to *feel* more confident start *looking* more confident.

For Advanced Players

- Focus on making birdies
- Do the Birdie Game. . .A LOT. It will teach more than you can imagine!

Exercise #7: Put It Into Practice

Take a few moments to review this section and try to implement one or two of the mental cues or games presented above. They should be a part of your weekly practice and/or daily habits. If you try to do all of them, you'll struggle to do any of them well. If you'd like more guidance, don't hesitate to contact me.

www.tcplaybook.com
Instagram: @tcplaybook
205.200.4686

"You'll never find the truth if you've already made up your mind about what it ought to be."

—Hank Johnson

FINAL EXAM: Go and Do It!

I HOPE YOU HAVE THOROUGHLY ENJOYED READING THIS BOOK and completing the assignments I have suggested. If you apply the principles that you've learned, I can guarantee you that you will improve your scoring average, have more lower rounds, less frustration, and simply enjoy the game as it was meant to be.

If you're one of the people to have read this far and haven't seen any improvement, let me pose three challenges and one encouragement: First, reread the book (the summaries at least) and complete the exercises *in their entirety* exactly as they are written. Second, you likely are working through the content with a clouded set of lenses due to your own bias. I have been there myself. Be sure you are reading it with a completely open mind. Third, *come and see me and my team as an individual or attend one of my classes*. I am confident I can get you shooting the lower scores you desire and explain any areas of confusion you have. I also want to encourage you to continue to redo some of the assignments and *give it time* for these principles to become a habit. These principles work for everyone that applies them, so give them time to take effect and understand that some of the lessons are designed to teach, not only what works, but what doesn't work as well.

My whole premise for writing this book and creating the classes was out of a passion to help golfers play better with the skill sets they have. If you want a different set of skills, then find an instructor who has a history of making golfers better and commit yourself to their instruction. I don't want you to have another round of golf where you felt like the round just got away from you. Put another way, I don't want your *rounds* to happen *to you,* I want *you* to happen *to your rounds*! While it is a game of chance, at the end of the day, you do have some say and control over how that plays out.

I also have a desire to help as many people as possible, and this book and the coursework was my way of doing that. If you follow the reading and exercises in order and continue to revisit them, you have set into motion a process of improvement that can't be stopped. You start with a small core number of beliefs and systems that continually build on one another like a snowball builds on itself as it rolls along the ground. This book is both scientific and heavily artistic in nature. Your brain can develop instincts that will be better than mine for you. It just needs a *new way of thinking* that will enable you to solve any problem you face, and maximize your learning as you develop your experience through both successes and failures.

If you are someone looking for specific answers, I'm sorry if I didn't directly provide the ones you were looking for. Understand that in order to give specifics, I would have to know you deeply. Take time to review the principles and apply them wherever you can. You will likely find your answer among the situations you face with the tools I have provided. If that still doesn't do it for you, *come and see me*. I'd be happy to answer your specifics and help you, as the old song goes, "Know when to hold 'em, know when to fold 'em."

To the high-level tournament golfers and coaches at all levels of play, the principles in this book apply to you, too. While you may already do many of these very well, I'm certain there are a few things that you can take away for yourself or your players that will make you or them better on average. (I learn something new every day). I know as well as you do that elite level golf carries with it a number of other skills that a player must manage and situations that he or she will encounter that require additional pieces of information. Unfortunately, this is beyond the scope of this book. As I learned from a wise friend of mine, "If you try to say everything about anything, you'll end up saying nothing!" If you want more assistance and more specifics that are not covered in this book, please give me a call. I also hope to provide a shorter "Players Guide" and "Coaches Guide" in the future that discuss these concepts. Until then, let's sit down, have a conversation, and get on the course together to take your game or your program to a whole new level!

Remember, at the end of the day there is only one question that matters, the question that guides all the decisions you'll ever make:

What Did You Shoot?

PRODUCTS

Go To Caddie®
Save 15%, discount code: tcplaybook
https://www.gotocaddie.com

Flaghunting®
Save 15%, discount code: TCPLAYBOOK
https://www.flaghunting.com

BirdieFire®
https://birdiefire.com

BlueGolf®
https://www.bluegolf.com

Google®
https://www.google.com

StrackaLine®
https://www.strackaline.com

ToughLies360®
https://toughlie360.com

Trackman®
https://trackmangolf.com

ACKNOWLEDGEMENTS

Thank you to the early adopters of this program, as you paved the way for countless others to enjoy golf at a whole new level! Thank you to my wife Rebecca, my parents, my students, my coworkers, fellow instructor and former LPGA Tour Player Siew Ai Lim, and my boss, friend, and mentor Hank Johnson for your review, edits, additions, challenging questions, and most of all, your love and encouragement to bring this book to fruition.

Thank you also to Jon Whithaus for your instrumental coaching at Ohio Wesleyan. I couldn't have imagined getting this far, but am proud and excited to hear of the hundreds and thousands of stories of golfers the world over who will enjoy the game, see the game, and play the game at the levels of which they've always dreamed. To all of the students who get to experience golf in this new way, thank you for helping to make this book a reality!

About the Author

Scott Hassee is a PGA Class A Teaching Professional who has been a golf instructor for 10 years. He began golfing at the age of 12, played throughout high school and, in college, joined the Ohio Wesleyan University golf team under Coach Jon Whithaus. He graduated in 2010 with a bachelor's degree in economics and a minor in mathematics. Upon graduation, he learned to teach under 2004 PGA National Teacher of the Year, Hank Johnson, at Greystone Golf and Country Club in Birmingham, Alabama.

As a multi-sport athlete in high school, Scott's love of math and his fascination with game theory developed. He designed and created a program incorporating both as a way to teach course strategy that is easy to understand and put into practice. He has taken concepts from the golf greats—players and coaches—on game management, putting a unique spin on playing better golf and shooting lower scores, which enable players to play better right out of the gate.

His students have won more than a dozen collegiate events (three of whom have become All-Americans). His junior golfers have won more than 200 events including several who have won state titles. As a coach with four TPI certifications, Scott has a passion for learning and helping his students get better, faster. He follows up by tracking the performance of his students every year to ensure they continue on their upward trajectory. His average student improvement in the course of a year is more than nine strokes. To him, if his students aren't improving, he's not doing his job.

For more information about
Scott Hassee and
The Champions Playbook visit:
www.tcplaybook.com
Instagram: @tcplaybook
205.200.4686

BIBLIOGRAPHY

Dr. Alistair Mackenzie. *Golf Architecture-Economy in Course Construction and Green-Keeping*. Coventry House Publishing. Dublin, Ohio. © 2015. Print.

Tom Watson with Nick Seitz. *Tom Watson's Strategic Golf*. NYT Special Services Inc. Trumbull, CT. © 1993. Print.

James Y. Bartlett and the Professional Caddies Association. *Think Like a Caddie Play Like a Pro*. Sellers Publishing, Inc. South Portland, Maine. © 2010. Print

Edward B. Burger and Michael Starbird. *The Five Elements of Effective Thinking*. Princeton University Press. Princeton, NJ. @ 2012. Print.

CPSIA information can be obtained
at www.ICGtesting.com
Printed in the USA
LVHW020948291020
669988LV00006B/8